This book is the result of a co-publication agreement between Anhui People's Publishing House (China) and Time AACP (Australia)

Chinese Folklore Culture Series – Festival
Author: Dong Qiang

ISBN: 978921816550
Ebook ISBN:
978-1-921816-92-5 ePub
978-1-921816-93-2 Kindle
978-1-921816-94-9 PDF

Published by:

TIME AACP
Expanding Horizons
www.aacpasia.com

An imprint of the ATF Ltd.
PO Box 504
Hindmarsh, SA 5007
ABN 90 116 359 963
www.aacpasia.com
Expanding Horizons

CONTENTS
目录

The Lantern Festival
元宵节 ······ 001

February Lunar II
二月二 ······ 010

The Tomb-sweeping Festival
清明节 ······ 019

The Water-sprinkling Festival
泼水节 ······ 028

The Dragon Boat Festival
端午节 ······ 037

The Chinese Valentine's Day
七夕节 ······ 049

The *Zhongyuan* Festival
中元节 ······ 060

Nadam Fair
那达慕大会 ······ 071

The Mid-Autumn Festival
中秋节 080

The *Chongyang* Festival
重阳节 091

The Winter Clothing Day
寒衣节 100

The Winter Solstice Festival
冬至节 110

The *Laba* Festival
腊八节 118

Chinese New Year's Eve
除夕 127

The Lantern Festival
元宵节

The Lantern Festival, a grand traditional festival which usually falls on the fifteenth day of the first lunar month, is another important festival after the Spring Festival. In many places, people regard Chinese New Year's Eve as the beginning of the Spring Festival season and the Lantern Festival as the end. Therefore, for many people, the Spring Festival season isn't over until the Lantern Festival. China is a country with a vast territory and a long history, and there are various customs such as having sweet dumplings, enjoying festival lanterns show, performing dragon and lion dance on the Lantern Festival.

元宵节是一个非常隆重的传统节日，一般在每年农历的正月十五日。元宵节是继春节之后，又一个重要的节日。在不少地方，人们将除夕认为是春节的开始，将元宵认为是春节的尾声。因而在人们看来，元宵节过后，春节也就结束了。中国幅员辽阔、历史悠久，元宵节的习俗也各有不同，主要有吃元宵、赏花灯、舞龙、舞狮等常见习俗。

Ⅰ.Origin

It is said that the origin of the Lantern Festival comes from Buddhist ceremonies. In the Buddhist doctrine, people compare the light of fire to the majesty of the Buddha. Buddhists usually put lamps to pay homage to the Buddha. On the 30th of every December in

一、来历

据说，元宵节的来历与佛教的宗教仪式有关。在佛教教义中，人们将火光比作佛祖的威严。在佛教中，教徒们通常要摆放灯具，以表达对佛祖的崇

Buddhist calendar, a grand ceremony of lighting lamps will be held to show their devout heart to the Buddha. By sheer coincidence, the day of Buddhist calendar falls on January 15th in the lunar calendar, so both Buddhists and ordinary civilians held grand celebrations. From then, the custom of enjoying lantern show was handed down to the public to become a common practice.

In the folk, there is another funny story about festival lanterns. A long time ago, ferocious beasts and birds attacked human and livestock everywhere so that people had to get together to fight against them. At that moment, a sacred bird landed on earth because of losing its way back, but it was killed by a hunter accidentally. On the death of the bird, the Jade Emperor was enraged so that he immediately gave an order that divine troops would descend from Heaven to make a fire to burn all kinds of beings on January 15th. The Jade Emperor's daughter was so kindhearted that she couldn't bear to see people suffer a lot without making crimes, so she risked her life to tell people the news by driving the auspicious clouds furtively. All of them were too scared to be at a loss at the news. An older man came out and said, "Take it easy, and we can

敬。在佛教仪式中，每年佛历的十二月三十日都要举行盛大的燃灯法会，以表达人们对佛祖的虔诚。佛历中的这一天正好是中国农历的正月十五日，因此寺庙与民间都要举行盛大的庆祝仪式。此后，元宵节张灯的仪式便传入民间，蔚然成风。

在民间，还流传着与花灯相关的有趣故事。传说在很久以前，到处都是凶禽猛兽，它们四处伤害人和牲畜，人们就组织起来去打它们。正在这个时候，有一只神鸟因为迷路而降落到人间，却不小心被猎人给打死了。玉皇大帝知道后，恼羞成怒，立即下旨，要求天兵天将于正月十五日这一天到人间去放火，将所有的生灵都通通烧死。玉皇大帝的女儿是一个心地善良的姑娘，他不忍心看到百姓们无辜遭难，于是便冒着生命危险，驾着祥云来到人间，将这个消息告诉大

decorate with lanterns and streamers, light firecrackers and set off fireworks to create a false impression which makes Jade Emperor believe that we all have died in the fire on January 15th of the lunar calendar." All the people agreed with him and then went to prepare separately. Not until January 15th in the lunar calendar, the Jade Emperor came to earth to inspect as expected. He found there was red glow and stupendous roar in the distance, which lasted for several days. The Jade Emperor believed that people must have suffered from enough punishment, so his grievance was eliminated involuntarily. People also felt very happy because they had protected their lives and property. In order to commemorate the victory, every January 15th in the lunar calendar, all families must hang lanterns and set off fireworks to commemorate such a wonderful day.

家。大家听说这个消息后，都吓得不知所措，不知道该怎么办。这时，有一个老人家站出来说话。他对大家说："不要慌张，正月十五日这一天，我们所有人家都要张灯结彩，点燃爆竹，燃放烟火。这样一来，等玉皇大帝来看的时候，就以为大家都被烧死了。"所有的人听到这个主意后，纷纷点头认同，于是便分头去准备了。到了正月十五日的这一天，玉皇大帝果然来到人间视察。只看见远处一片红光，响声震耳欲聋，而且连续好几天都是如此。玉皇大帝认为人间已经遭受了惩罚，怨气也就消除了。人们也十分高兴，认为已经保住了自己的生命与财产。为了纪念这次成功，每到正月十五日的时候，家家户户都要悬挂灯笼，通过燃放烟火来纪念这一美好的日子。

Ⅱ.Customs

In the folk, there are various kinds of activities, like guessing lantern riddles, eating sweet dumplings, enjoying festival lanterns, performing dragon and lion dance, etc..

Lantern Couplet

Vertical written couplets on lanterns are the so called Lantern Couplet. On Lantern Festival, people will go out to enjoy a great variety of colorful lanterns. The couplets are written on some lanterns. Throughout history, a lot of scholars and poets have written many popular and readable poems which could be put on the lanterns to express their pleasant feelings.

Festive Lanterns

A festive lantern is a traditional folk artifact and also an important symbol in Chinese traditional culture.It originated from worshiping events in *Han* Dynasty, and later became an entertainment project. When the Lantern Festival comes every time, people living in palace will hold a grand ceremony from dawn to dusk. Every corner of the palace will be placed a lighted lantern for lighting. Later on, lighting lanterns became popular as one part of

二、习俗

在民间,元宵节这一天有各种各样的活动,主要有猜灯谜、吃汤圆、赏花灯、舞龙、舞狮等。

灯联

所谓灯联,就是写在灯上的对联。元宵节的这一天,人们要纷纷外出去欣赏各式各样的花灯。花灯的种类很多,其中一些花灯上还写有对联。从古至今,不少文人骚客留下了许多脍炙人口的诗歌,他们将诗歌书写在花灯之上,以表达自己愉悦的心情。

花灯

花灯是一种传统的民间手工艺制品,是中国传统文化的重要符号。花灯最初源于祭祀活动,后又发展为一种娱乐项目。花灯最早产生于汉代。每逢元宵节的时候,皇宫总要举行盛大的庆祝活动,而且从深夜一直举办到天明。为了能够照明,于

the Lantern Festival. There are a lot of different kinds of colorful lanterns, and the themes of the lanterns are mainly airy pavilions and pagodas or flowers, birds, fish and insects, which are dyed into different colors such as red, yellow, green & blue, etc.. In ancient China, people did not only enjoy the lanterns but also had an activity of guessing lantern riddles. Usually, people wrote the riddles on the lanterns and invited the pedestrians to guess the answers. Whoever gave the correct answer would receive a nice gift. It was also a good opportunity for the young to date in enjoying the lantern show. Some girls would describe their sweethearts as riddles on the lanterns to make people guess. In some places, it was very popular to take in a son-in-law by guess-

是在皇宫的各个角落都要点上灯笼。此后，灯笼作为元宵节的一部分，由此盛行开来。花灯的形式各种各样，不仅色彩斑斓，而且款式较多。花灯的内容多以亭台楼阁、鱼虫花卉等题材为主，所染制的色彩，有红、黄、绿、蓝等多种颜色。在中国古代，元宵节这一天，人们不仅赏花灯，而且还要举行猜灯谜的活动。大家将谜语写在花灯上，然后请过往的行人来猜。如果猜中的话，便会得到精美的礼物。灯会同样是青年男

ing lantern riddles. Girl' s parents would hang the lantern riddles in an eye-catching position of the street and invited young men to guess the riddles. Parents would betroth their daughter to the guy who can answer the riddles successfully.

Having Sweet Dumplings

The sweet dumpling is a kind of Chinese snack, one of those which have the longest history. It originated from *Song* Dynasty when its craftsmanship was easier. People just needed to chop fruit, twisted the glutinous rice flour like a ball and put the chopped fruit inside. You cannot eat the ball until it is boiled. Later on, the crafts manship was becoming more and more complicated and the dumpling was stuffed with not only fruit but also sesame, almonds, walnut, rose and sweetened bean paste. While tasting the sweet dumplings, people will make soup with white or red sugar. In many places, it is popu-

女约会的好去处。有的女孩子，还将自己心目中的如意郎君，用谜语的形式写在灯笼上，让大家来猜。还有的地方流行猜灯谜、招女婿的活动。女方的父母，将灯谜挂在街上醒目的位置，然后邀请青年人来猜。如果谁猜中的话，他们就将自己的女儿许配给谁。

吃汤圆

汤圆是中国历史最悠久的小吃之一，最早起源于宋代。那个时候，汤圆的制作工艺还比较简单。人们将水果剁碎，然后用糯米粉搓成球，将水果放入球内，煮熟后便可食用。后来，汤圆的制作工艺越来越复杂，不仅用水果作馅，而且芝麻、杏仁、核桃、玫瑰、豆沙等都可以制作成馅。吃汤圆的时候，需要用白糖或者红糖熬制成汤。不少地方还流行吃油炸汤圆。所谓油炸汤圆，就是将汤圆放到锅里油炸，然后食用。还

lar to have fried sweet dumplings, which are fried in oil then eat. In other places, sweet dumplings are rolled instead of twisting.

有的地方，汤圆并不是手工捏成的，而是滚出来的。

Eating Refreshments

Besides sweet dumplings, there are some other traditional refreshments to eat. Noodle is a necessity for northern Chinese people on the Lantern Festival. Every evening (on that festival), all the family members sit at the table and talk with each other happily while eating delicious noodles, symbolizing constant joys. In the south of China, people are fond of eating the rice cake which is a kind of common food steamed with rice flour. It signifies "to be promoted every year", which means that people make improvement in work and life year by year. Moreover, people in some places will eat a kind of barley pancake, which is named after the meaning of a happy reunion.

吃糕点

元宵节除了吃汤圆外，还要吃一些传统的点心。在中国的北方，面条是元宵节必备的点心。每逢元宵节的那天晚上，一家人围坐在一起，一边聊着开心的事情，一边吃面条。吃面条表示喜庆绵绵不断的意思。在南方，人们喜欢在元宵节这天吃年糕。年糕是民间常见的食物，用米粉蒸制而成。年糕的意思，就是"年年高"，比喻人们在工作和生活中，一年比一年有所提高。此外，有的地方在元宵节这一天，要吃一种大麦做成的饼，取名"大团圆"的含义。

Lion Dance

Lion dance is a folk art with Chinese characteristics and also the symbol of Chinese traditional culture. While on Lantern Festival or some other grand ceremonies come, people must invite each other to perform lion dance together for pleasure. The activity of lion dance originated from the period of Three Kingdoms. At that time, Buddhism was just introduced into China, thus, the Buddhist culture greatly influenced China accordingly. After long period of development, the activity of lion dance has been deeply rooted in the Chinese culture and become a part of it. There are a variety of performing forms of lion dance. With the music (accompaniment), performers will wear lion masks and act as a lion to perform a lot of different shapes. It is said that the performance has the function of getting rid of evil.

舞狮

舞狮是中国特有的民间艺术，也是中国传统文化的象征。每逢元宵佳节或举行盛大的庆典仪式时，人们就要相邀在一起举行舞狮活动，来增添欢喜的气氛。舞狮这项活动，起源于三国时期。那个时候，佛教刚刚传入中国，因此佛教文化也随之影响中国。经过长期的历史发展，舞狮活动已经深深地植根于中华文化之中，成为中国文化的一部分。舞狮的表演形式也多种多样。在表演者的音乐伴奏下，人们头戴狮子面具，扮演成狮子的样子，做出狮子各种各样的形态。据说，这种表演有驱除邪恶的作用。

Land Boat Dancing

Land boat dancing is also an particular folk art. It was said that in order to commemorate the achievements of *Dayu*'s succeeding in controlling the floods, people hold the performance of land boat dancing. The land boat is not a real one but a model made of bamboo.

划旱船

划旱船也是一种独特的民间艺术。传说为了纪念大禹治水的功绩，民间要举行划旱船的表演。旱船并不是真的船，而是用竹子制成一种船形框架，

Then the bamboo frame would be wrapped up by the colored cloth, tied around girls' waist. Generally, the performers are females who

need to sit in the boat model with wooden oars, assuming the rowing posture. In some places, people are singing beautiful songs while rowing (a land boat) to express their best wishes for a happy life.

然后将船用彩布围缀，套在姑娘的腰间。表演者一般为女性，他们坐在船中，手里拿着木桨，做出划行的姿势。有的地方，还一边划，一边吟唱优美的歌曲，以此表达人们对幸福美好生活的祝愿。

February Lunar Ⅱ
二月二

February Lunar Ⅱ is a traditional festival celebrated on February 2nd of the lunar calendar. There are various folk activities on that day and it is also named Green Grass Treading Festival, Spring Dragon Festival and Dragon-head-raising Festival.All kinds of recreational activities will be held at the arrival of the festival, especially the grand dragon dances.

二月二是中国传统的民间节日，一般在每年农历的二月初二举行。二月二节有许多风俗活动，又名“踏青节”、“春龙节”、“龙抬头节”等。每逢这一节日来临，人们都要举行各种娱乐活动，尤其是举行盛大的舞龙表演。

Ⅰ.Origin

As a folk saying goes, “The Dragon King will give rain to the universe on February 2nd in the Chinese lunar year by raising his head.” February Lunar Ⅱ was called *Zhonghe* in ancient China. According to a legend, the Dragon King would raise his head for rain every lunar February 2nd. The Dragon King was the supernatural being who was in charge of cloud and rain in the ancient Chinese legend, so that it would be rainier and rainier after February 2nd. Dragon-head-raising means, after hiber-

一、来历

民间的俗语说：“二月二，龙抬头。”二月二节，古代称之为“中和节”。相传，每逢农历二月初二的时候，都是龙王抬头的日子。龙王是中国古代神话中，主管云和雨的神仙。二月二日一过，雨水会逐渐增多。所谓龙抬头，指的是经过冬眠，各种虫子开始渐渐苏醒，万木复

nation, insects would come back to life and plants would begin to grow. Thus, February Lunar II is also called Spring Dragon Day. The reason why people wish the dragon to raise his head is that dragon symbolizes prestige. It is believed that dragon can overawe the insects. If the dragon raises his head, the insects will be frightened to hide themselves somewhere. People expect that the dragon can overawe the reviving insects to secure a harvest, as well as the booming of people and their livestock. At the same time, people begin to plant rice seedlings on February Lunar II. It is also called Spring Cultivating Day because the warm spring falls into cold winter, the ground begins to melt, which is a good season for cultivation in spring. It is said that if the universe doesn't come back to life, the booming thunder will awaken it.

苏，所以这天又被称之为"春龙节"。人们之所以希望龙抬头，是因为"龙"是威望的象征。人们相信，龙对昆虫具有威慑作用。龙抬头，则意味着昆虫都会害怕地躲藏起来。人们希望龙能够震慑蠢蠢欲动的虫子，以祈祷农业丰收、人畜兴旺。这一天也是农民开始插秧、播种的节日。严寒的冬天即将过去，温暖的春天即将来临，大地开始解冻，天气逐渐转暖，这正是春耕的好时节，所以又称之为"春耕节"。据说，如果这一天世间万物还没有苏醒的话，那轰轰隆隆的雷声将会唤醒大地。

II. Customs

People would celebrate the coming February Lunar II by holding all kinds of activities. In northern part of China, on the very morning of February Lunar II, every family will go to the wells or rivers to fetch water with lighting lanterns. After returning home, people will burn incense, offer sacrifice to

二、习俗

每当二月二节时，人们要举行各种活动来庆祝节日的到来。在中国的北方，二月二节这天清晨，家家户户都要早早地提着灯笼前往井口边或河边挑水。返回家中后，

mourn their ancestors, and also hang the lanterns high on the top of the door frame to show happiness. In addition, people will cook a variety of delicious foods to treat friends and relatives. Interestingly, all the foods cooked on that day must relate to the Chinese character of dragon.

Dragon-whisker-like Noodle

The dragon-whisker-like noodle is a popular food in northern China with long and thin shape in appearance, like dragon's whiskers. There exists the custom of eating drag-

on-whisker-like noodles every February 2nd of the Chinese lunar year. Another story is also popular in the public with dragon-whisker-like noodles. It is said that in the *Ming* Dynasty, an emperor lost appetite for any food because he was in a bad mood. The ministers worried too much, seeing the emperor being thinner and

人们要烧香、摆放供品、祭祀祖先，将灯笼高悬于门梁之上，以示喜庆。这一天，人们还要做各种美味可口的食物，招待亲友与来宾。有趣的是，这天所做的各种食物，都与"龙"字有关。

龙须面

龙须面是一种流行于中国北方的食物。从外观看，是一种又细又长、形似龙须的面条。每年农历二月初二的时候，人们就有吃龙须面的风俗。民间还流传着与龙须面有关的一个故事。相传在明代的时候，有个皇帝因为心情不好，对任何食物都没有胃口。眼见皇帝一天天消瘦下去，大臣们都心急如焚。就在这个时候，有个刚进宫的厨子，毛遂自荐要做道菜让皇帝品尝，希望能讨皇帝欢心。大臣们对这个新厨子不屑一顾，但是眼下没有更好的办法，于是同意了他的请求。晚上，皇帝用膳的

thinner. Then a newly employed chef volunteered to cook a dish to satisfy the emperor. But ministers looked down upon the chef, they had no choice but agree to his request. In the evening when the emperor began to have meals, the chef placed the food into a big bowl. The emperor asked the eunuch around, "What' s this? I don' t want to eat. Withdraw it." The chef said to the emperor, "What is placed in the bowl is your country." On hearing this, the emperor was very curious, so he uncovered the bowl to find ordinary noodles in it. The emperor blamed angrily, "Aren' t they the ordinary noodles? Why do you call it my country? I will punish you unless you explain it clearly today!" The chef kneed down and said, "My majesty, the noodles in the bowl are not ordinary at all, but the country of the *Ming* Dynasty like the endless noodles live on for ever. What's more, the noodles are just like dragon' s whiskers, and they can be eaten only by the real emperor." The emperor was delighted very much with good appetite to eat the noodles while appreciating and praising with a great pleasure.

时候，厨子将食物装入一个大碗中。皇帝问身边的人："这送来的是什么，我不想吃，撤下去吧！"厨子对皇帝说道："皇上，这里面装的是江山社稷。"皇帝听后，很好奇，于是将碗打开一看，原来装的就是普通的面条。皇帝对厨子生气地说道："这不就是普通的面条吗？怎么叫江山社稷？如果你今天不说个明白，我就要惩罚你！"厨子赶忙跪下说道："皇上，这里面装的不是普通的面条，希望我大明朝的江山，就像这面条一样，延绵不断，永远长久。皇上，这面又像是龙的胡须，只有真龙天子才能享用这面条。"皇上听后十分高兴，于是胃口大开，边品尝，边赞赏，龙颜大悦，赞不绝口。

The Food Related to Dragon

A lot of foods eaten on February Lunar II relate to dragon. The spring pancake eaten this day is called eating dragon's scales; the rice eaten this day is named dragon's sons; the wonton eaten this day is called eating dragon's eyes; the dumplings eaten this day is called eating dragon's ears. What's more, people will eat a thin kind of pancake. In legend, it was thought that February Lunar II was the birthday of the Dragon King in Eastern Sea, so eating pancakes was to eat Dragon King's afterbirth and chew Dragon King's disasters; throwing pancakes referred to bury Dragon King's afterbirth. People hoped to awaken the dragon to pray for their health and safety by relating food to dragon. However, there were some taboos on dragon. In some areas, women couldn't use needles for clothing because it might hurt dragon's eyes. In some places, people couldn't wash clothes because they might make dragon's skin injured. On the very beginning of the morning, after getting up, people would hold lanterns to light up their houses' beam, murmuring while lighting, "Lighting up the house beam on February Lunar II will drive scorpions and centipedes away."

与"龙"有关的食物

二月二节这天，人们吃的许多食物都与龙有关。人们在这天吃春饼，民间叫"吃龙鳞"。人们在这天吃米饭，民间叫"吃龙子"。人们在这天要吃馄饨，民间叫"吃龙眼"。人们在这天要吃饺子，民间叫"吃龙耳"。这天人们还要吃摊煎饼。在民间，人们认为二月二是东海龙王的生日，吃煎饼就是吃龙王的胎衣。吃煎饼，是为了咀嚼龙王的灾祸。扔煎饼，是为了埋葬龙王的胎衣。之所以人们将食物的名字与龙联系在一起，就是希望唤醒龙，以此保佑人们健康平安。当然，这天也有许多与龙有关的禁忌。有的地方，妇女们在这天不能使用针线，害怕伤害了龙的眼睛。有的地方，人们在这天不能洗衣服，害怕伤了龙皮。在这天清晨，人们刚起床的时候，还要打着灯笼照亮房梁，边照口

Eating Pig' s Head

In ancient China, people would lay pig' s head as the sacrifice to gods when they had magnificent mourning activities. Pig' s head couldn' t be eaten at usual time. People could only eat it on December 23rd, the Preliminary Eve after a busy and hard year for ordinary families, butchering pigs and sheep for feasts. From the Preliminary Eve to the Lantern Festival, people could eat pork as extra meals. Especially, on the Chinese New Year' s Eve, the whole family would get together to have a reunion dinner, including dumplings. After 15th of the first lunar month, the pork left was not much, only leaving the pig' s head which could be eaten just on February Lunar II. The Dragon King took charge of falling rain, so peasants had to offer the best sacrifices to him to pray for a better harvest and luckier life in the following year.

里还要念叨："二月二照房梁，蝎子与蜈蚣无处躲藏。"

吃猪头

在中国古代，每当举行盛大祭祀活动的时候，人们都要摆上猪头，作为供奉上天的祭品。平常的时候，猪头是不能随便乱吃的。一般在平常的百姓家中，人们忙忙碌碌地辛苦一年，只有到年终腊月二十三过小年的时候，才能杀猪宰羊。从小年开始，一直到元宵节，人们都可以吃肉，改善伙食。尤其在除夕夜的时候，家人围聚在一起吃团圆饭，吃饺子。正月十五过后，家中的猪肉也吃得差不多了，只剩下了一个猪头。这个猪头只能在二月二才能吃。龙王是掌管降雨的，所以农民要将最好的祭品供奉给龙王，希望一年都能风调雨顺、事事如意。

Inviting the Married Daughters Home

Gunainai is an address for the married daughters in folk China. On every lunar February 2nd, the married daughters would return their parents' home for a reunion celebration. On the morning of this day, the relatives of their parents' family would get up early and do a thorough cleaning of the house to greet their daughters. Different places share different customs, but similar general procedures. In Chinese folk tradition, the married daughters are not allowed to stay at their parents' home even one day in lunar January. They have to go back to their husbands' home after visiting her parents on the very day. After February Lunar II, however, she could stay at her parents' home for days or half a month. During February Lunar II, the married daughters could relax herself at her parents' home after a busy preparation for Spring Festival dinner at her husbands' family. When February Lunar II comes, she can visit their childhood playmates and chat casually. Because their parents are usually so kind that they seldom let their married daughters to do housework.

接姑奶奶

姑奶奶，是中国民间对已经出嫁了的女儿的一种称呼。每逢二月初二的时候，出嫁的女儿要返回娘家，与父母团圆。所以，二月初二这天清晨，娘家的人就要早早起来，将屋子打扫干净，准备迎接女儿回家。各地接姑奶奶的风俗略有不同，但大体程序相同。在中国人的传统习俗中，正月时，已出嫁的女儿是不能回娘家住的。正月初二去娘家拜年后，也必须当天赶回婆家，不能留宿。但到了二月初二，女儿就可以回娘家住，并且可以住上好几天，甚至半个月。因为出嫁的女儿在过年的时候，在婆家忙碌了很长的时间，帮助婆家准备年夜饭，所以，当到二月初二的时候，女儿就可以返回娘家好好休息一下。出嫁的女儿回到娘家后，父母一般不让她做家务事。她们也正好趁着这段时间走亲访友，寻找儿时的玩伴，轻松愉快地聊天。

Ploughing Work

On February Lunar II, the royal court would hold a significant activity, namely, the emperor would go out of the imperial palace to show how to plough himself, because it was warm enough in the north part of China, and it was right time to cultivate in spring. The emperor would symbolically lead officials to hold a grand ploughing ceremony to persuade peasants not to delay the cultivating time. The important cultivating ceremony showed that the imperial court paid much attention to farming. During the period of the *Ming* Dynasty and early *Qing* Dynasty, the emperor generally

耕田

二月初二这天，宫廷要举行一项重大的活动，那就是皇帝要亲自去京郊外耕田。每逢二月初二的时候，北方已经进入了春暖花开的时节。寒冷的冬季已经过去，这时正值春耕大忙的时节。为了不耽误农时，劝导农民及时耕种，皇帝这天要象征性地率领文武百官去京郊外举行盛大的春耕仪式。春耕的仪式十分重要，充

held cultivating ceremony outside of imperial court in the Temple of Agriculture near *Beijing*. In the ceremony, the emperor would symbolically plough the fields. After Emperor *Yongzheng* of *Qing* Dynasty, the cultivating ceremony was changed to be held in the Summer Palace.

分展现了朝廷对农耕的重视。明朝与清朝前期的时候，皇帝一般在京城的先农坛举行春耕仪式。皇帝会象征性地耕地松土。清朝雍正皇帝以后，春耕的仪式改在圆明园举行。

The Tomb-sweeping Festival
清明节

The Tomb-sweeping Festival, also known as Green Grass Treading Festival, Willow Leaf Inserting Festival, usually begins around April 5th of the Gregorian calendar. It is not only one of the twenty-four solar terms in the lunar calendar, but also an occasion for Chinese to offer sacrifices to their ancestors. Falling on the sunny and fresh spring, it is a good time for spring outing. Various sport activities would be held in ancient times on that day.

清明节，又名“踏青节”、“插柳节”，多在每年公历的4月5日。清明，不仅是农历二十四节气之一，还是中国人祭祀祖先的节日。清明节正值阳光明媚、吐故纳新的春季，因而成为人们春游、踏青的好日子。古时候的人们在清明这一天，要举办各种体育活动。

Ⅰ. Origin

Dating from the *Zhou* Dynasty, the Tomb-sweeping Festival has a history over 2 500 years. The ancient Chinese almanacs recorded the origin of the word *Qingming*. *Qingming* means everying is growing in a clean and bright atmosphere and they can feel the fresh sunshine in spring. From the growing period of the crops, the Tomb-sweeping Festival comes at a time of when everything comes back to life,

一、来历

清明节始于周代，距今已有2 500多年的历史。中国古代的历法书，记载了“清明”一词的来历。清明，指的是万物的生长清洁、明净，能感受春天清新的阳光。从农作物的生长周期来看，清明节正值万木复苏之际，也

and it is the right time to begin ploughing and sowing. 108 days have passed since the Winter Solstice last year. The Chinese believe that the lucky number 108 represents completeness, peace and eternity, predicting everything bidding farewell to the cold winter and entering a warm spring.

There are two arguments telling the origin of the custom of tomb-sweeping on the Tomb-sweeping Festival. One tells that it originated in memorial service of emperors and evolved over a period of years into worshiping ancestors on Tomb-sweeping Festival. The other tells that Tomb-sweeping Festival gradually evolved into a day for worshiping ancestors due to the influence of the Cold Food Day, the day before Tomb-sweeping Festival, which is a time for sacrifice and tomb sweeping.

是春耕播种的时节。清明节距离上一年的冬至节正好108天。在中国人的观念中，108代表着圆满、祥和、久远，是一个吉祥的数字，预示着万物从寒冷的冬季进入温暖的春天。

清明扫墓习俗的来历，据传有两种说法：一说源于古代帝王将相的“墓祭”仪式，后来民间多效仿；二说清明节的前一日即寒食节，就是祭祀、扫墓的时节，清明节受寒食节的影响，逐渐演变为祭祖的节日。

Ⅱ. Customs

There're varieties of folk customs on Tomb-sweeping Festival, such as sweeping tombs to worshiping ancestors, going to the countryside for travel, playing on the swing, playing *Cuju*, planting trees, flying a kite, inserting willow branches, forbidding fire, etc..

二、习俗

民间在清明节这一天有许多丰富多彩的节日习俗，如祭祖扫墓、出游踏青、荡秋千、踢蹴鞠、植树、放风筝、插柳叶、禁火等。

Sweeping Tombs and Offering Sacrifices

The Tomb-sweeping Festival is an important day for Chinese to worship and memorize the ancestors. Tomb sweeping, usually called *Shangfen*, is an activity offering sacrifices to the deceased. Tomb sweeping is not limited to that day, three days before or four days after the Tomb-sweeping Festival is all acceptable, as it is recorded in the folklore. And this rule of time is made for the convenience of people who are about to worship ancestors. On that day, people bring their kids and the elders, taking fruit, food, drink, joss paper and spirit objects with them to the graves. People will put

祭祀扫墓

清明节是中国人祭祀祖先的节日，是祭奠先人、缅怀故人的日子。扫墓，俗称"上坟"，是一种祭祀亡故者的活动。祭扫的时间并不限于清明节当天，在前三天或后四天之内均可。民间还流传着"清明朝祖，前三后四"的说法，据说之所以这么规定，就是为了方便人们前去祭扫。在上坟的那一天，人们要携带瓜果酒食、冥钱、冥品，一家人携

offerings in front of the graves, burn joss paper, add new earth to the grave, engrave the fuzzy scripts of the tombstone, cut off branches of willow to insert on the grave and then they will kowtow to worship the ancestors.

老扶幼前往亡故者的墓前祭拜。人们将供品摆放在墓前，再将纸钱焚化，为坟墓盖上新土，为墓碑篆刻描字，并折下几枝嫩绿的柳枝插在坟上，然后行叩头祭拜礼。

Spring Outing

Spring Outing, also called *Tanchun*, is a custom handed down from ancient times till now. People appoint to go for an outing to appreciate the beautiful scenery on the 3rd day of the 3rd lunar month, so Tomb-sweeping Festival is also called March Festival in ancient times. It is time to see a bright sunshine, splendid flowers and lush trees and grass. After worshiping, the relatives and friends go together to the countryside for climbing, boating, or having a picnic, to enjoy the wonderful spring.

出游踏青

踏青，又名“探春”，是从古至今流传下来的习俗。在农历的三月份，即农历的三月三日，人们相约前往郊外去欣赏大自然的美好风光，古时候又称之为“三月节”。清明正值阳光明媚、百花争妍、草木复苏的时节。这一天，亲朋好友在祭祀完先人后，便结伴前往郊外游玩，有的相约爬山，有的泛舟水上，有的结伴野炊，从而共同感受美好的春天。

Playing on the Swing

A swing is a kind of games which refers to the one that two ropes are tied to a fixed frame and both the ends of ropes are closely tied a board at the bottom, people will be able to swing back and forth on the board.

荡秋千

秋千是一种将长的绳子系在固定的架子上，下面挂上蹬板，人随着蹬板来回摇动的游戏用具。

In the northern part of our country in the Spring and Autumn Period, there was a custom of playing on the swing on the Tomb-sweeping Festival. At that time the ropes were made of leather, and then branches were used as the frame, with ribbons decorating on both sides. As children's favorite activity, playing on the swing can encourage them to be brave and also make them healthy.

Playing *Cuju*

As a sport activity created by the Chinese, *Cuju* is recognized universally as ancestor of modern soccer due to their similarities. And then it prevails in many countries, such as North Korea, Japan, Vietnam, etc.. *Cuju* is a ball which is made of leather. It is said that the emperors created this game for the purpose of training soldiers'. As one military training item, the game started to popularize in various parts of China in the Spring and Autumn Period. And it was deeply loved by the people from the bottom to the top in *Han* Dynasty. In a normal *Cuju* game, players were divided into two teams, and each team had twelve players, the winner would be decided on the goals kicked by each team.

春秋时代在我国的北方，人们就有清明节荡秋千的习俗。当时拴秋千的绳索多用兽皮制成，后来改用树枝为架，并在两侧用彩带装饰。荡秋千是儿童们最喜爱的活动，可以锻炼小孩勇敢的精神，也是增进健康的有益活动。

踢蹴鞠

踢蹴鞠是中国人发明的一项体育活动。蹴鞠与现代的足球运动相似，被世界公认为足球的始祖，后来在朝鲜、日本、越南等国家十分流行。蹴鞠是一种用皮革制成的球。相传，踢蹴鞠是中国皇帝为了训练士兵而发明的一种运动。春秋战国时，踢蹴鞠作为一项军事训练项目，已经在各地广泛流传开来。汉朝的时候，上至王宫贵族，下至平民百姓，都十分喜爱蹴鞠这项运动。比较正规的蹴鞠比赛，一般分为两队，双方各有十二名队员参加，以踢入球门的球数的多少来决定胜负。

Planting Trees

The Tomb-sweeping Festival is in a period for trees growing and farmers' spring plowing and seeds sowing. The warm sunshine and continuous spring rain makes it the best time to plant trees. Therefore, people have a habit of planting trees on the Tomb-sweeping Festival.

Flying Kites

Flying kites is one of the activities people enjoy, and the Chinese was the first to play this game. A kite at the early period was made of wood, therefore, it was called *Muyuan* (wooden kite). Wood was replaced by bamboo and silk in *Han* Dynasty. Later, paper was used to make a kite. Thus, *Muyuan* (wooden kite) was renamed *Zhiyuan* (paper kite).

Elders and children enjoy themselves by

植树

清明节是植物生长的时节，也是农民春耕播种的时节。和煦的阳光，春雨绵绵，正值培植树木的最佳时期。因此，在清明节的时候，人们有种植树木的习俗。

放风筝

放风筝是清明节人们所喜爱的活动。风筝最早是由中国人发明的，初期的风筝是用木头所制，故名“木鸢”。汉朝时，木头被竹子和丝绸所替代，后来又改用纸张，“木鸢”也因此改名为“纸鸢”。

每逢清明时节，老年

flying kites when Tomb-sweeping Festival coming. They flied kites not only in daytime but also at night. In the dim moonlight, people hung small colorful lanterns, named God's Lantern, on the thread, like the shining stars. After flying the kites up to the sky, people would snip the thread and let the wind take the kite up. It is said that if the kite was sent to the ends of the earth, it would bring good luck, erase evil and cure illness.

人与儿童以放风筝为乐。人们不仅白天在郊外放风筝，而且在夜晚也放风筝。在月色朦胧的深夜，人们在挂风筝的线上，挂上一串串彩色的小灯笼，宛若闪烁的星星一般，被称为“神灯”。古时候的人们，将风筝放入蓝天后，便剪断牵线，任凭清风吹拂，据说是为了将风筝送入天涯海角，以祈求祛病消灾，给人们带来好运。

Inserting Willow Branches

Inserting willow branches is performed on the Tomb-sweeping Festival. Most people usually inserted willow branches into the lintel while people in other places put willow leaves on their heads or put hats knitted by willow branches on children's heads. One saying is that this custom was established in memory of the common ancestor of the Chinese nation — *Shennong*. There is another saying that willow leaves inserted into the lintel was for weather forecasting. As the old Chinese proverb says: It will be rainy if the willow branches are green and it will be sunny when you see the branches dried. According to the third saying, inserting willow branches can help people

插柳叶

清明节有插柳叶的风俗，最盛行的便是将柳叶插在门楣上。也有不少地方，将柳叶戴在头上，或是用柳条编织成帽子，戴在儿童的头上。插柳叶的风俗，一说是为了纪念中国人的祖先神农氏。二说在清明节的这一天，人们将柳枝插在屋檐下，据说可以预报天气。中国古代的谚语有：柳条青，雨蒙蒙；柳条干，晴了天。三说清明节插柳条，有辟邪的功效。清明本是祭祀亡

ward off bad luck. The Tomb-sweeping Festival, one of the three biggest Chinese Ghost Festivals, is a day to offer sacrifice to the deceased. To thwart the harassment of ghosts, willow branches are inserted and worn. The legend of willow originated from Buddhism. The Avalokitesvara, who is familiar to many Chinese people, always carry a bottle with willow branches in the hand. The Avalokitesvara wets the branches with some holy water in the bottle and waves the willow branches to bless everyone on the earth and eliminate illnesses and disasters.

故人的节日，是中国的三大鬼节之一。这一天，人们为了防止鬼的侵扰，纷纷插杨柳、佩戴杨柳，以防鬼上身。杨柳辟邪的传说，源于佛教思想。中国人所熟悉的观世音菩萨，在她的手中就握有一瓶，瓶内便插有杨柳。观音用杨柳沾上瓶内的圣水，便可赐福众生、消除疾病与灾祸。

Shooting Willow

Shooting willow was a game for training archery skills in ancient times. According to historical records, warriors in groups went to the countryside for archery practice. A pigeon was put into a calabash, then the calabash would be hung on the willow branches high. One bended the bow to shoot the calabash and then the pigeon would be free to fly away. The height pigeon flied would determine the outcome.

射柳

射柳是古代一种练习射箭技巧的游戏。据古代的历史文献记载，清明节的这一天，武士们趁着阳光明媚的春天，结队来到郊外，练习射箭。他们将鸽子放入葫芦之中，然后将葫芦高高地悬挂在柳树上，用弯弓射葫芦，如果射中，鸽子便展翅飞翔，以鸽子飞的高度来判别胜负。

Cock-fighting

Cock-fighting, an incredibly popular recreation on the Tomb-sweeping Festival,

斗鸡

斗鸡是清明节十分盛行的一种游戏。斗鸡这

lasted from the Tomb-sweeping Festival to the end of Summer Solstice. Cock-fighting was quite popular in the *Tang* Dynasty, when emperors as well as civilians were all involved in the activity.

项娱乐活动，从清明节开始，一直持续到夏至日结束。唐代的时候，斗鸡成风，不仅民间斗鸡兴盛，而且皇帝也经常在宫廷中斗鸡。

The Water-sprinkling Festival
泼水节

As a festival with a strong ethnic features of the *Dai* Nationality and one important day for other minorities in *Yunnan*, the Water-sprinkling Festival is as important as the Spring Festival. Also known as Phi Ta Khon Festival, the Water-sprinkling Festival is celebrated in the mid-June of the *Dai* calendar or tens days before or after the Tomb-sweeping Festival, and usually lasts for three or four days.

泼水节是傣族最富有民族特色的节日，也是云南其他少数民族重要的节日，其重要性与春节一样。泼水节又称“佛诞节”，时间是傣历的六月中旬，即清明节前后的数十天，节期一般为3～4天。

Ⅰ.Origin

The Water-sprinkling Festival originated from India. It came out from a Brahmanic ritual in its early time, and later it was absorbed by Buddhism. In the 12th century, the Water-sprinkling Festival was introduced into *Dai* people area in *Yunnan* through countries of Southeast Asia by spreading Buddhism. There are many beautiful legends in folklore about the origin of the Water-sprinkling Festival. It is said that there was an dissolute and cruel monster who had committed many towering crimes

一、来历

泼水节源于印度，最初源于婆罗门教的一个宗教仪式，后又为佛教所吸纳。公元12世纪，泼水节随佛教的传播，经东南亚诸国传入我国的云南傣族地区。民间有许多关于泼水节来历的美丽传说。据说在很久以前，有一个荒淫残暴的魔王在西双版纳为非作歹。一

in *Xishuangbanna* long long ago. One day, having robbed eleven beautiful girls, he went to rob the twelfth girl, the cleverest and the most beautiful one, she decided to save herself and got rid of this monster for all the people. One night, she made the monster drunk and pretended to say with flattery, "Your honor, you are so strong that I don't think there is anything which will hurt you!" It gave him so much satisfaction that he himself imparted the secret that he would be killed as long as he was hanged with a piece of his hair. The words were firmly fixed in her mind. On that night, watching the monster was asleep, she quickly cut off a piece of his hair from the monster's head with care, put it around his neck, and tightened it until he died. The moment the head fell off the monster's shoulders down onto the ground, it burned instantly, which could only be put out when the head lifted off the ground. No matter where the head be thrown, there would always be fire. In their anxiety, the twelve girls had to hold the head in turns in case the fire spreaded. When one of the girls carried the head, other girls must sprinkle water to her to wash away blood on her body. After fighting for days and nights, the fire of evil was finally put out by the brave girls. And the people of *Xishuangbanna* had

天，魔王抢了十一个美丽的姑娘。之后，他又去抢来了第十二个姑娘。这个姑娘不仅是最美丽的一位，也是最为聪慧的一位。她决定自救的同时，为老百姓除去这个魔王。一天夜里，这个美丽的姑娘将魔王灌醉了，奉承地说道："大王，您本领如此高强，世上应没有什么可以伤害你了！"魔王颇为得意地说道："那倒是！不过，只要用我的一根头发勒住我的脖子，我也就没命了。"姑娘于是暗自记住，待魔王呼呼大睡之后，小心翼翼地拔下魔王的一根长发，将他勒死了。但糟糕的是，魔王的脑袋落到地上后，即刻燃起了熊熊大火，只有将他的脑袋拎起来，火才能熄灭。魔王的脑袋无论扔到哪儿，都会燃起大火。情急之下，十二个姑娘只能轮流抱着魔王的脑袋以防火势蔓延，其他的姑娘就在旁边为抱着魔头的

picked up the peace and happiness again. Later, *Dai* people commemorate the beautiful, brave girls in the form of sprinkling water each New Year in *Dai* calendar.

姑娘泼水，以冲刷她身上的血污。夜以继日地奋战之后，邪恶的火终于被英勇的姑娘们所扑灭。西双版纳的百姓们，重新过上平静的生活。后来，傣族人民每逢傣历新年，便以泼水的形式纪念这些美丽而又勇敢的姑娘们。

Ⅱ.Customs

The Water-sprinkling Festival, which has the meaning of seeing off the old and welcoming the new same as the Chinese New Year's Eve, usually lasts for three or four days. Various activities such as Buddha bathing, sprinkling water, dragon boat race, throwing pouches, letting rise and lighting *Kongming* lantern up are held during the festival.

二、习俗

泼水节的节期一般为3～4天。泼水节在傣语中的意思名为"送旧迎新"，与除夕相同。

泼水节期间要举办许多丰富多彩的活动，主要有浴佛、泼水、赛龙舟、丢包、放高升、放孔明灯等。

Buddha Bathing

On the first morning of Water-sprinkling Festival, pious people all take a bath, put on clean, colorful clothes and come to temples to worship the Buddha. A pagoda is piled up in the temple with sand by people who will then sit round the pagoda and listen to the preaching

浴佛

泼水节的第一天清晨，虔诚的人们沐浴更衣，身着彩服，纷纷至寺庙拜佛。人们还会在寺院里用沙堆砌一座宝塔，然后围绕着"塔"环坐，聆听佛

of Buddhists. A statue of Buddha will be placed in the yard at noon, and clean water will be brought to prepare for the rites of Buddha bathing, which means to wash away the dust of the statue with clean water.

教僧侣讲经诵法。中午时分，人们将一尊佛像置于院内，担来澄澈的清水，施行“浴佛”礼，即用清水为佛像洗去尘埃。

Water Sprinkling

Water sprinkling, the most solemn activity comes on the second day of the Water-sprinkling Festival. People believe that the sprinkled water symbolizes happiness, health and good luck and it can ward off illness and misfortunes. So as far as they are concerned: The more the better. The water sprinkling can be divided into two types: gentle sprinkling and wild sprinkling. The gentle sprinkling is a form for the elders, whose collar will be

泼水

泼水节的第二天，便迎来了最隆重的“泼水”活动。民间认为，所泼之水是象征幸福、健康、吉祥的水，可以消灾祛病。所以，应该泼得越多越好。当然，泼水亦有所讲究，有“文泼”与“武泼”两种分别。“文泼”，指的是对长者的泼水形式，泼

opened and a spoon of water will go along his back, with blessings. The wild sprinkling lets people sprinkle freely. As the sprinkling starts, people will carry buckets and basin filled with water, which will be used in sprinkling when people see each other, at that time, the street will be full of cheers and laughters.

水时舀起一勺清水，一边说着祝福语，一边拉开对方的衣领，好让水沿着脊背流下去。“武泼”则没有这么多的讲究，就是尽情地自由泼洒。泼水开始之时，人们或担着水桶或捧着铜钵、脸盆纷纷拥到大街小巷，逢人便泼洒清水，一片欢声笑语。

Dragon Boat Racing

A dragon boat race will be held on *Lancang* River on the second day of the Water-sprinkling Festival. It is the wooden dragon boat decorated with colorful flowers, it is so striking and extremely festive. What's more, there are also wooden boats in the shape of a peacock or a big fish. Dozens of rowers including men and women sitting in the boat row very heartily to strive for the goal. The moment the game starts, huge crowds of people come to both sides of the river. Cheers, applauses and exciting beatings of gongs and drums deafen the ear. The winners will get their prize at the platform and then a grand banquet will be held.

赛龙舟

泼水节的第二天，还要在澜沧江上举行划龙舟比赛。龙舟是木制的，上面装饰有彩花，格外鲜艳，显得十分喜庆。此外，也有仿效孔雀或大鱼形象的木船。赛船上一般坐有数十名男女桨手。比赛开始之时，赛手们便奋力划桨，向终点冲刺而去。两岸的观众人山人海，人们的欢呼喝彩声与欢快激奋的锣鼓声震耳欲聋。获胜的龙舟赛手们，将到主席台前领取奖品，并且还要举行盛大的宴会。

Throwing Pouches

There is an extremely romantic game to

丢包

丢包是傣族未婚青

throw pouches, and the game for unmarried young men and women paying court to each other. As a token of love for men and women, the well-made pouch, which is usually filled with cotton seed, is decorated with colorful spikes of flower. The game goes like this: Yong men and women stand respectively in lines on the green lawn, young girls throw the pouches to the young men they admire, and then young men throw the pouches back to young girls. The affection is transferred through pouches.

年男女相互求爱的一种游戏，极富浪漫色彩。包是由未婚女性用花布所精心编制而成，四角缀着五彩的花穗。包里面一般装有棉籽。包指的是男女双方的定情信物。丢包游戏是这样的：男女青年在绿茵茵的草坪上各站成一排，姑娘将做好的包掷给自己心仪的小伙子，然后小伙子再掷回给姑娘，以包传递感情。

Letting Rise

Letting rise refers to one kind of the *Dai* fireworks made of a long bamboo by the *Dai* people. Gunpowder is filled at the root of a two meter long bamboo pole, which is then placed on a high shelf built with bamboo. After that, it is lighted and the bamboo will fly rapidly in the sky like a rocket, creating a pretty firework display. The letting rise usually takes place at night. The higher the letting rise flies, the more prouder people in the village will feel, as it symbolizes to have a bright future.

放高升

高升是指傣族人用长竹竿自制的一种傣式烟火。在一根两米多长的竹竿根部填上火药，然后将其放置在竹子搭成的高架子上，点燃火引。竹子便嗖嗖地如火箭般飞上高空，旋即爆出灿然绚丽的烟火。傣族一般在夜晚放高升，高升飞得越高越远的寨子，寨子里的人也觉得更加光彩，寓意将拥有美好未来。

Lighting up *Kongming* Lanterns

The *Kongming* lantern is one kind of ob-

放孔明灯

孔明灯是一种高约6

long lantern with the height of six meters and the diameter of two meters or so. Late in the evening, people take *Kongming* lanterns, gather at the public square and light the candles in the lanterns. The smoke generated has created the buoyancy which can let the *Kongming* lantern rise up slowly. Flammable oilskin can also be hung under the lanterns, which makes the sky as bright as the day even at night. The *Kongming* lantern is a symbol of bright future and good luck. People make blessings and prayers to the lanterns, hoping that their wishes will come true one day.

米、直径约 2 米的长圆形大灯笼。入夜时分，人们带着孔明灯齐聚于广场，点燃灯里的蜡烛。灯笼内便充满烟气，利用其产生的浮力，孔明灯便腾空冉冉升起。在灯笼下方也可挂着可燃油布，夜空被这一盏盏的孔明灯照亮得如同白昼一般。孔明灯有光明与吉祥的寓意，升入高空的孔明灯寄托着人们的美好愿望，人们对着孔明灯进行祈祷与祝福，希望自己的愿望能早日实现。

Peacock Dance and Elephant-foot Drum Dance

The beautiful dance is usually arranged on the third day of the Water-sprinkling Festival. Regardless of gender and age, people dress up themselves and gather at the square of the village, singing, dancing with the instrumental accompaniment, and laughing heartily. The beautiful, attractive peacock dance gains the cheers and a big applause from the people. While dancing the elephant-foot drum dance, the dancers need to dance in a circle with pas-

跳孔雀舞与象脚舞

泼水节期间自然少不了优美的舞蹈，一般安排在节日的第三天。无论男女老少，人们都身着盛装，齐聚到村寨的广场上，在乐器的伴奏下，载歌载舞、尽情欢笑。优美动人的孔雀舞，引来了人们大声的喝彩与掌声。跳象脚舞的时候，需要跳舞者围成一个圆圈，一同热

sion and nuttiness, Singing loudly enough to create an exciting.

Ganbai

The *Ganbai* of *Dai* people is the same as going to the temple fair. A grand *Ganbai* rite will be held during the Water-sprinkling Festival every new year of the *Dai* calendar. The most famous one takes place in *Xishuangbanna, Yunnan. Ganbai* activities will be held in every cities, towns and villages from April 12th to April 19th each year. People rush to the spot of *Ganbai* and choose the goods they are fond of.

Having Barbecue

During the celebration of Water-sprinkling Festival, traditional *Dai* foods will be made by every family, such foods with ethnic flavor as roast fish are their choices, and the most famous two among them are *Haolosu* and *Haohuo*. *Haolosu* is made with glutinous rice flour, brown sugar and fragrant flowers, which is wrapped in small parcels with leaf of banana. After being steamed, it is edible.

情、潇洒地舞蹈，同时嘴中还高声吟唱，发出动人的旋律。

赶摆

傣族人的赶摆与逛庙会一样。每逢傣历新年的时候，人们便要在泼水节期间举行隆重的赶摆仪式。云南西双版纳地区在泼水节所举行的赶摆最为有名。一般从每年的4月12日延续到4月19日，在每个县市、乡镇或村寨都会举行赶摆活动。人们纷纷从各地赶到赶摆的现场，挑选自己心爱的物品。

吃烧烤

人们在过泼水节之时，各家均要制作传统的傣族食物，还要吃烤鱼等民族风味食品，尤以“毫咯素”与“毫火”最为著名。毫咯素的制作方法即用糯米粉加上红糖，以及一种名叫咯素的香花，再用芭蕉叶包成小包，蒸熟

While making *Haohuo*, one makes steamed glutinous rice and pound it into pulp, then they will be put together with brown sugar and made into the shape of a disk. And it will be edible after being dried and baked or fried.

了即可食用。毫火是用蒸熟的糯米饭舂捣至烂，加些红糖，做成圆片状，待晒干后用火烤或油炸后即可食用。

The Dragon Boat Festival
端午节

As one of the three Chinese traditional festivals, the Dragon Boat Festival has been spread so far for over a thousand years. Influenced by this festival, people in all places of East Asia have had the tradition of celebrating the festival, with their own national factors. People in China do not know which is right and which is wrong on the origin of the Dragon Boat Festival. People in *Jing-Chu* celebrate this festival for the sacrifice of *Qu Yuan*, while people in Three-*Jins* in memory of *Jie Zhitui*, and people in *Wu-Yue* area believe this festival is associated with *Wu Zixu*. So when did this festival start and how many moving stories were associated with it?

端午节是中国传统三大节日之一，流传至今已逾千年。东亚各地受中华文化影响不仅有过端午的习俗，而且各国还融入本民族元素。即便是华夏故土，各地对端午起源也莫衷一是。荆楚百姓过端午意在祭奠屈原，三晋人民过端午实则纪念介之推，吴越民众则认为端午与伍子胥有着深厚的渊源。那么，端午节究竟滥觞于何时？又深藏着哪些娓娓动人的传说呢？

Ⅰ.Origin

Prehistoric ancients who regarded rice as the staple food and made a living by such agriculture as rice and wheat planting had paid close attention to season solar terms.The fifth

一、来历

饭稻羹鱼的史前先民，世代以水稻、小麦等农业生产为生，对时令节气十分关注。阴历五月初

day of the fifth lunar month is the most important busy farming season. The origin of the festival had something to do with agriculture. People had the custom of bathing in *Lancao* soup on the Dragon Boat Festival, therefore, the Dragon Boat Festival is also called the *Lan* Bathing Festival. Furthermore, it was called the *Tianzhong* Festival in *Tang* and *Song* dynasties, and it was called the May Festival and the Daughter's Festival in *Ming* and *Qing* dynaities. And the opinions of its origin vary widely.

五，是夏季中最重要的农忙时节。可见，端午的起源最早与农业生产有关。古人在端午这一天，有用兰草汤沐浴的习俗，故端午节别名"沐兰节"。唐宋时，亦称"天中节"。明清时，称之为"五月节"、"女儿节"等。有关端午的起源，各种传言众说纷纭。

The Festa Celebrated with Totem

It is said that the Dragon Boat Festival was originally a festival for the dragon. It was recorded in *Strategies of the Warring States* that people in *Wu-Yue* area had the custom of cutting off hair and having a tattoo to act like the descendants of the dragon. The dragon is accepted as the totem for people in *Wu-Yue* area. As the most important activities, both dragon boat racing and having *Zongzi* have something to do with the dragon: The boat used in the racing is the dragon-shape boat and the *Zongzi* thrown into the river is often eaten by the dragon. In order to battle against natural disasters and have favorable weather in the coming year, our ancestors had such sacrificial activities as dragon sacrifice, dragon boat rac-

图腾祭日

相传端午原本是龙的节日。《战国策》中就载有吴越百姓多"断发文身"、"以像龙子"的遗俗。龙是吴越百姓尊奉的图腾。端午节中最重要的节日项目——竞渡和吃粽子都与龙相关，竞渡用的是龙舟，而粽子投到水里又常被蛟龙所窃。为了抵御自然灾害，祈盼来年风调雨顺，先民在端午这天有举行龙祭、划龙舟、吃粽子、焚香点烛、供果献牲等祭祀活动。

ing,having *Zongzi*,burning incense and lighting candles, and offering fruits and livestock,etc.

Offering Sacrifice to *Wu Zixu*

Wu Zixu was originally a man from the state of *Chu*. His brother and father were sentenced to death penalty due to jealousy. In order to run away from being involved in the case, he rushed to the State of *Wu* at the very night. He was appreciated for his outstanding talents by *Helü*, the king of the State of *Wu*. He helped the king a lot in such great undertaking of founding a state as attacking the State of *Chu* and *Yue*. *Helü* died because of the wounds he received in the war, therefore, *Fuchai*, his son succeeded. Under the help of *Wu Zixu*, *Fuchai* thrashed the State of *Yue*. *Goujian*, the king of the State of *Yue* paid a substantial bribe to the prime minister of the State of *Wu* to make peace while resting his troops in the *Kuaiji* Mountain. *Wu Zixu* knew well that the armed forces of *Yue* would rise up again so he advised the king not to breed calamities for the future and to wipe out the country *Yue* to stamp out the root of trouble. But *Fuchai* had implicit faith in slander, he agreed to make peace with each other and then began to estrange *Wu Zixu*. The king of the State of *Yue* knew that only the death of *Wu Zixu* could restore his kingdom. *Fuchai* was

祭伍子胥

伍子胥原为楚国人，父兄因遭猜忌被楚平王所杀。伍子胥为避祸株连，连夜逃至吴国。因伍子胥才华出众，很快便受到吴王阖闾的赏识。他帮助吴王伐楚攻越，成就宏图大业。吴王在伐越中负伤而亡，其子夫差继位。夫差在伍子胥的辅佐下为父报仇，大败越国。越王勾践一面栖兵会稽山，一面用重金贿赂吴国丞相请求议和。伍子胥深知越国必兴兵再起，遂力谏不可养痈遗患，理应乘势灭越。夫差偏信丞相谗言，同意议和，此后遂逐渐疏远伍子胥。越王深知伍子胥不除，复国必遇险阻。勾践在重贿吴王近臣后，夫差猜忌伍子胥，并赐剑令其自刎。伍子胥临终前断言吴国必亡于越。夫差闻言大怒，于五月五日将伍子胥的尸首投于

suspicious and jealous of *Wu Zixu* due to believing the words of his other close courtier, who received a substantial bribe from *Goujian*, so he made *Wu Zixu* commit suicide. Before his death, *Wu Zixu* declared that the State of *Wu* would be subjugated by the State of *Yue* inevitablely. Hearing his words, *Fuchai* was so angry that he ordered someone to drown *Wu Zixu*'s body to the river. People in the State of *Wu* respected him so much that they retrieve his body from the water and buried him under the ground in *Xukou* (today's *Suzhou* in *Jiangsu* Province). Later, people of *Wu* and *Yue* Kingdoms regarded *Wu Zixu* as the God of River, and the God of Wave. They built a memorial temple to enshrine him and the tradition of offering sacrifice to *Wu Zixu* has been handed down.

胥江。吴国百姓十分敬重和缅怀伍子胥，遂将其尸首打捞上来，埋在胥口（今江苏苏州）。此后，吴越人民奉伍子胥为江神、波神，还专门供奉有伍相祠，祭祀伍子胥的风俗遂延传至今。

Tribute to *Qu Yuan*

As the minister of King *Huai* of *Chu* in the Spring and Autumn Period, *Qu Yuan* advocated the policy of appointing people by their political integrity and ability, making the country rich and building up a strong troop, and making a resistance to the State of *Qin* under the combination with the State of *Qi*. Unfortunately, he was opposed by the nobilities like *Zilan* and removed from his position and exiled. On his way to exile, such imperishable

悼念屈原

屈原是春秋时期楚怀王的大臣，他倡导举贤授能、富国强兵，力主联齐抗秦，遭到贵族子兰等人的强烈反对，后被革职流放。他在流放途中，写下忧国忧民、千古绝唱的《离骚》、《天问》、《九歌》等不朽诗篇。不久，秦军攻破楚国都城，屈原眼

poems concerning about his country and people were written and ranked as a masterpiece throughout the ages as *Lisao*, *Tianwen*, and *Jiuge*. Soon after, the *Qin* army made a breakthrough to the capital city of *Chu*. Watching the dishonors of his motherland, the mentally exhausted man drowned himself in the *Miluo* river after writing the last work *Huaisha* on the fifth day of the fifth lunar month. The man of lofty sentiments and aspirations for the beloved country commanded the respect of people in the State of *Chu*. People who surrendered themselves to grief went to the river to pay their last respect to him.Fishermen drove the boats to search for his bodies desperately in the river. The Rice and vegetable rolls prepared for *Qu Yuan* were thrown into the river

见自己的祖国遭受凌辱，心力交瘁，遂于五月五日写下绝笔《怀沙》后，毅然自投汨罗江而捐躯赴国。他满腔爱国的壮志豪情，深受楚国百姓敬佩。百姓们哀痛不已，自发前往江边凭吊。渔夫们划起小舟，在江上拼命寻觅屈原的尸首。有位渔夫拿出为屈原准备的饭团投入江中，说是喂饱鱼虾蟹，而不吞噬屈原的身躯。一位老郎中，端来一坛雄黄酒洒入江中，说是醉倒蛟龙水兽，以免伤害屈原。后来，百姓们便以划龙

by a fishman wishing that the fishes, shrimps, and crabs would not consume *Qu Yuan*'s body after being fed. An old doctor sprinkled the realgar wine into the river to turn all aquatic beasts drunk so that *Qu Yuan*'s body would not be hurt by them. From then on, such customs as dragon boat racing, eating *Zongzi* and drinking realgar wine are held in memory of the great patriotic poet.

舟、吃粽子、饮雄黄酒等习俗来祭奠屈原这位伟大的爱国诗人。

Ⅱ.Customs

The Dragon Boat Racing

It is said that, people living in the areas of *Jing-Chu* and *Wu-Yue* all had held the tradition of boat racing, which was derived from the memory of *Qu Yuan* and *Wu Zixu*. People in *Wu-Yue* had always had the custom of dragon boat racing since ancient times. After the king of *Yue* State took the throne of *Wu* State, he showed great compassion for the death of *Wu Zixu* and honored *Wu Zixu*'s loyalty for the king of *Wu* State. He not only built an alter and killed white horses, constructed a temple near the river, but also advocated the people to race, dragon boats in respect for *Wu Zixu*. Thus, it

二、习俗

龙舟竞渡

相传，荆楚、吴越的百姓都有端午竞渡的风俗。追溯源头，与纪念屈原、伍子胥有关。吴越百姓自古有龙舟竞渡的遗俗。越王勾践灭吴后，十分敬重伍子胥的忠烈，对伍子胥的谗杀表示深深

has had a custom of worshipping *Wu Zixu* even in the original *Yue* State. During the Epoch of Warring States, *Yue* State was taken over by *Chu* State, and the tradition of boat racing spread due to the expansion of its boundaries of the *Chu* State to memorize *Qu Yuan* who killed himself by jumping into the *Miluo* River.

Having *Zongzi*

Having *Zongzi*, namely, rice dumpling wrapped in reed leaves. According to *records in Custom and Geographical Environment*, which was compiled by *Zhou Chu* in the *Wu* State in the dynasty of Three Kingdoms, people living in the south regions of the *Yangtze* River wrapped broomcorn millet with *Gu* leaves, boiled them in heavy lye, which would make them thoroughly cooked, and then ate them on May 5th and the Summer Solstice. Moreover, people named them *Zongzi* or rice dumplings. This is by far the earliest record of *Zongzi*. *Wu Jun* in the *Liang* of Southern Dynasty also recorded in *Xu Qixie Ji* that the *Chu* people mourned *Qu Yuan* with

的怜悯。他不仅立坛杀白马，祭子胥，筑庙于江上，还在越国倡导竞渡，以致原属越的地方都有祭伍之举。战国时越国被楚国所灭，吴越竞渡的风俗随着楚国疆域的拓展，遂遍布南方，荆楚人民借竞渡纪念投汨罗江的屈原。

吃粽子

据三国东吴周处所著的《风土记》记载，江南"俗以菰叶裹黍禾，以淳浓灰汁煮之，令烂熟，于五月五日及夏至啖之，一名粽，一名角黍"。这是迄今为止有关粽子最早的记录。南朝梁代吴均在《续齐谐记》中也记载，楚人哀屈原"每贮米竹筒报祭"。江南是最早种植水稻的地区之一，糯米的栽培甚早，江南有煮粽的传统也就不足

rice in bamboo tube every time when the day came. The south of the *Yangtze* River is one of the regions where rice grew at the earliest time. Cultivating of glutinous rice is even earlier. There is no wonder that people there have the tradition of eating *Zongzi*. Up to now, *Zongzi*, which remains local flavor in *Jiaxing*, *Zhejiang* Province, has gained popularity both at home and abroad.

为奇。至今浙江嘉兴的粽子仍是本地特色小吃，风靡海内外。

Tugging Various Grasses

The so-called grass tugging means that there are two persons tugging with grass tendon and the one whose end is broken will fail in the game. There appeared a poem called *Fuyi* in *National Customs: Zhounan of the Book of Songs*, telling the custom of women and children playing tugging grasses. The funny story of *King Wu* and *Xishi* tugging various grasses was recorded in the book of *Zhongwu Jiwen*. Plantain seeds, which are frequently used in grass tugging, also got the name of court grass in southern dialect.

斗百草

所谓斗草，就是两人用草筋互相拉扯，被扯断的一端作输。《诗经·国风·周南》篇中就有"芣苢"一诗，讲述了妇孺嬉戏斗草的风俗。在《中吴纪闻》一书中，则记载了"吴王与西施尝斗百草"的趣事。斗草常用"车前子"，南方方言称之为"打官司草"。

Hanging Folium Artemisia Argyi

In the ancient people's opinion, May is a month full of evil things, and people need to collect herbal medicines to get rid of bad luck. Therefore, the belief of hanging folium artemisia argyi to drive out evil spirits and pray for good health during the Dragon Boat

挂艾叶

先民认为，五月是恶月，要采集草药，攘除晦气，所以各地有端午挂艾草驱邪，祈愿身体健康的说法。民间传说，艾叶能灸治百病，故端午挂于门

Festival was popular everywhere. Folk legends say that folium artemisia argyi can cure various illnesses. For this reason, it is hung in front of the doors for the purpose of dispersing bad luck of the family and blessing good health of the family members.

前，可以驱散家中晦气，保家人身体安康。

Winding *Baisuo*

Winding *Baisuo* means twining colored silk threads on arms to avoid evil things. China, which is renowned in both ancient and modern times for its rich production of silk, started to breed silkworms to spin silk at a very early time. Colored silk thread is a type of silk of high quality, which is twined by people on arms during the Dragon Boat Festival with the name of *Pibing*, praying that people will not get entangled with epidemic diseases.

缠百索

缠百索是用五色丝线缠于臂上以避邪。中国以盛产丝绸享誉古今，很早就养蚕纺丝。五色丝线是一种材质较高的丝绸，端午节时百姓们将五彩丝系于臂，名曰辟兵，祈祷人们不被病瘟纠缠。

Drinking Realgar Wine

People drink realgar wine or spread it on children's face between forehead and ears and nose. Realgar, which is glossy and orange and also named as *Jiguanshi*, is frequently used in traditional Chinese medicine as a kind of detoxicant antidote and insecticide. In particular, it can drive away the pests such as centipedes and vipers etc.. The records also ap-

喝雄黄酒

端午时，百姓喝雄黄酒或用雄黄酒涂于小儿额头与耳鼻间。雄黄也称为鸡冠石，有光泽，呈橘黄色，中医常用此作解毒杀虫药，尤其可以驱逐蜈蚣、毒蛇之类的害虫。明崇祯时期的风俗志中亦

peared in custom ethnography, which was compiled during *Chongzhen* year of the *Ming* Dynasty, that evil things could be driven away by drinking realgar wine, spurting it in the room everywhere, and spreading it on the arms and foreheads of children.

有"饮雄黄酒，遍洒室中，点小儿臂额，以去毒"的记载。

Giving Fans

The custom of giving fans during the Dragon Boat Festival was prevalent in the *Tang* Dynasty. When sending out presents for the Dragon Boat Festival, single young men would give the most precious fans to their sweethearts. Most residents of *Chang'an* City in the *Tang* Dynasty gave fans with pendants as presents, and the market became the fan market during the Dragon Boat Festival. There were feather fans, silk fans and sandalwood fans etc.

赐扇

唐代流传端午赐扇的习俗。未婚青年男子，在送"端阳礼"之时，要将最宝贵的扇子送给情人。唐代长安市民在端阳时多互相馈赠坠扇，端午节期间集市变成扇市。扇类有羽毛扇、绸缎扇、檀香扇等。

Zongzi Games

In imperial palaces of the *Tang* and *Song* dynasties, a large number of dough dumplings, which needed to be made before the Dragon Boat Festival, were used for people to shoot with small horn bows, and those shot were expected to be eaten by the shooters. Among the ordinary people, the following game was popular during the Dragon Boat Festival: People unfastened leaves of *Zongzi* to compare their lengths, and the one who had the longest

粽游戏

唐宋宫廷中，端阳节需赶制许多粉团粽子，让人用小角弓去射，谁射中那只就吃那只。在民间则盛行比粽叶长短的游戏。端阳节时，人们解下粽叶对比长度，长者为胜。

leaves would become the winner.

Eating Eggs Boiled with Garlic

Every time it comes to May 5th, housewives in the villages of Central China get up quite early. They boil eggs together with garlic prepared in advance, and some even add several folium artemisia argyi, and then the whole family eat the boiled eggs for breakfast so as to avoid the five poisonous creatures and seek for physical fitness.

食大蒜蛋

中原等地的乡野村间，每逢端午节，女主妇起得特别早，他们将事先准备好的大蒜与鸡蛋放在一起熬煮，有的还在煮大蒜和鸡蛋时再放置几片艾叶，然后一家人早饭便食用煮熟的鸡蛋，以图避“五毒”，强身健体。

Hanging Acorus Calamus

Acorus calamus,which is a type of herbaceous plants, about forty centimeters high, primarily grows among gravels in mountains and enjoys the function of refreshing oneself, making body unimpeded and sterilizing due to the volatile oils it contains. When it comes to May 5th, people make calamus leaves in the shape of a treasured sword, and then hang them at the eave so as to turn calamities into blessings. Some people even bathe in the water boiled with acorus calamus for the purpose of getting rid of illnesses.

悬菖蒲

菖蒲是一种草本植物，高 40 厘米左右，喜生长于山间石砾处，含有挥发性香油，有提神通窍杀菌的作用。每逢端午，人们将菖蒲做成宝剑形的蒲剑悬于屋檐处，以图逢凶化吉。有的还用菖蒲烧水洗澡，以祛病疫。

Sticking Pomegranate Blossoms in the Hair

From the 1st to 5th of the fifth lunar month, every household in the north regions of *Ming* Dynasty dresses up little girls by wearing

簪榴花

明代端午节时，北方的民众从五月初一至初五，家家打扮小闺女，佩戴榴花于鬓发两旁以作

pomegranate blossoms in hair on the temples as articles for personal adornments. Therefore, it is also called the Daughters' Festival. Prior to the Dragon Boat Festival, newly married women need to visit parental home, which is called evading the Dragon Boat Festival.

饰物，因此，端午节又被戏称为“女儿节”。新嫁女子在端午节前，还要回娘家，称为“躲端午”。

The Chinese Valentine's Day
七夕节

The Chinese Valentine's Day, also named *Qiqiao* Festival, Seventh of July, Girl's Day and Sunbathing Book Day, is a festival whose theme is love, just like Valentine's Day of the western culture, so it's named Chinese Valentine's Day.

七夕节，又名"乞巧节"、"七月七"、"女儿节"、"晒书节"，是一个以爱情为主题的节日。七夕节类似于西方的情人节，人们又称之为"中国的情人节"。

Ⅰ. Origin

The Chinese Valentine's Day came from a lovely romantic story. Long long ago, in a village called *Niujiazhuang*, there was a clever, honest and handsome young man called Buffalo Boy, who lived with his brother and sister-in-law after his parents died. He was hard-working and kind-hearted to his neighbours, however, his sister-in-law referred to him as the ball and chain of the family. She abused him a lot and gave him a lot of work to do. Once in a late autumn, the sister-in-law forced the Buffalo Boy to pasture cattle in order to send him away, so she gave him nine heads of

一、来历

七夕节的由来，源自一个美丽动人的爱情故事。很久以前，在牛家庄有一位聪明、憨厚的英俊青年，人们称他为牛郎。他与邻为善、待人诚恳、吃苦耐劳，可惜父母早亡，只能与哥哥嫂嫂相依为命。嫂嫂为人狠毒，认为牛郎是家中的拖累，于是经常虐待他，逼他干很多活。一年深秋，嫂嫂为了撵走牛郎，逼他去放

cattle to pasture and told him, "If you could not bring ten heads of cattle home, otherwise you do not come back." The Buffalo Boy left, whooping his cattle out of the village and went into the deep forest. When he was sitting under a tree, broken-hearted, thinking about how to turn nine heads of cattle into ten, a white-bearded old man walked towards him and asked what was troubling him gently. Having heard his words, the old man smiled and told him, "Don' t be sad. There is an old cattle which is hurt in the *Funiu* Mount, and you can go to take good care of it. Once it is cured, you can take it home."

牛。临行前给他九头牛，嘱咐牛郎需变成十头牛时才能返回家中，否则就永远不要踏入家门半步。牛郎无奈，只得赶着九头牛出了村。牛郎独自一人赶着牛，进入了深山密林之中。他伤心地坐在树下，冥思苦想，不知何时才能赶着十头牛返回家中。这时，有一位白发胡须的老者来到他的跟前，和蔼地问牛郎因何事愁苦。牛郎一五一十地将自己的遭遇告知老者，老者听后笑着对牛郎说："别难过，在伏牛山里有一头受伤的老牛，你细心照顾它并帮它医治好伤，待老牛病愈后，你就可以赶着它回家了。"

Followed the old man' s instruction, the Buffalo Boy had more difficulty in finding an injured and hungry cattle. After having some fresh grass brought by the young man, the cattle raised its head and told him that he once was an immortal. He was the gray cattle Nilta-

牛郎遵照老者的指引，跋山涉水终于找到了那头受伤的老牛。牛郎见老牛饥肠辘辘，于是从山中打来最嫩的鲜草，细心地喂养它。待吃饱后，老

va in the heaven in the past. He was degraded from the heaven into the human's world due to breaking a few rules of the heaven. And he broke his leg carelessly, so that he had to stay here for few days. The old cattle told the boy that he could only be cured by the dew on hundreds of flower petals early in the mornings. Thus, the Buffalo Boy started to take care of the old cattle.He got up early in the morning to collect the dew on hundreds of flower petals. A month later, the cattle was healed. Then the Buffalo Boy brought his ten heads of cattle home. The sister-in-law, who thought he could never make it, was very surprised to see him coming home. She was still very reluctant to let him stay home, and began to think of ways to get rid of him. Every time she tried something to harm the boy, the old cattle always found his way to save him. At last, the spiteful woman got furious and banned him from coming back home again.

牛才微微地抬起头告诉牛郎，它原本是天界的灰牛大仙，因触犯了天规被贬入凡间，不小心摔坏了腿，无奈只得躺在这里好几日。老牛告诉牛郎，自己的伤口需用百花集结的露水清洗数日后才能痊愈。牛郎不畏辛劳，每天很早起来去收集百花的露水。经过一个月的细心照料后，老牛终于康复了，牛郎便高高兴兴地牵着十头牛返回家中。嫂嫂见到牛郎十分惊讶，原以为牛郎知难而退，不敢回家。见到牛郎将十头牛牵回来了，嫂嫂很不情愿地继续让牛郎待在家中。但是嫂嫂却始终怀恨在心，有几次都意图加害牛郎，却被老牛设法相救。嫂嫂无计可施，遂大发雷霆，狠心地将牛郎赶出家门，不准他再回来。

The Buffalo Boy started to live together with the aged cattle. Watching him being so lonely, the cattle came up with an idea, which was to help him marry a fairy from the heaven

牛郎只能与老牛相依为命。老牛见牛郎孤苦伶仃，十分可怜，于是便想出一个计谋，协助牛郎

and have a happy life. One day several fairies came from the holy palace to have a bath in the milky way. Each one of them is not only lovely but also beautiful. When they were enjoying their bathing, the Buffalo Boy who hid himself in the reed suddenly ran out and stole a fairy's clothes. The startled fairies got dressed in a hurry and flew away, only leaving the Weaver Girl whose clothes had been taken away by the Buffalo Boy. Under explicit instructions from the cattle, the young man expressed his affection to the fairy and asked her to marry him. Considering that he was so honest and righteous, the fairy, who is Weaver Girl, agreeably consented to his proposal of marriage. In order to help the couple live a happy life, the old cattle sneaked into the holy palace and risked his life to steal the silkworm eggs, mulberries, looms and weaving equipment for them. The pair of lovers got married and soon the fairy gave birth to their children, living a truly happy life. After years, the old cattle got sick and died long before. Before the cattle died, the Buffalo Boy was

娶天宫的仙女为妻，过上幸福的生活。一日，一群仙女从天宫来到银河沐浴，仙女们个个婀娜多姿、娇艳动人，她们在水中嬉戏，有说有笑。这时，早已藏在芦苇中的牛郎突然跑了出来，偷走了织女的衣裳。惊惶不安的仙女们很快穿好衣裳飞走了，唯独剩下织女。在老牛的授意下，牛郎对织女表达了爱慕之情，恳请娶织女为妻。织女见牛郎是一位憨厚、忠实的俊俏郎，于是便满口应诺。为了帮助牛郎夫妇过上幸福的生活，老牛不顾个人安危，从天宫偷来蚕种、桑葚、织布机、织布梭。两人结婚后，牛郎与织女过着男耕女织的快乐生活。两人相亲相爱、相偎相依，生活幸福美满，织女还为牛郎生养了一对儿女。后来，老牛因患疾病，

told by the cattle that he must take good care of his wife and should flay the cattle's skin since it would be of immense use eventually. After the cattle's death, the couple did as the cattle told and buried him in the mountain with great pains.

The fact that the Buffalo Boy and the Weaver Girl were married without the permission of parents was soon known to the Heavenly Emperor and Queen Mother of the holy palace. The Queen got so furious that she ordered to bring the fairy back to get punished. Though with great sympathy, the other Gods could do nothing but take the fairy away from the Buffalo Boy while he was out. After the Buffalo Boy came home and found his wife missing, soon he realized that she must be taken back to the holy palace. He put on a pair of shoes made of the cattle's leather right away and carried his two kids together with his shoulder pole to chase after his wife. Watching that he was about to catch up with the Weaver Girl, Queen Mother immediately pulled off a golden hairpin from her head and created a gap in the milky way to stop the Buffalo Boy. The clear milky way became muddy in an instant, and it stopped the steps of the Buffalo

一病不起，不久便死去了。临终前,老牛嘱咐牛郎要善待织女,并要牛郎将自己的皮剥下来,到危难之时定能派上用场。老牛病逝后，牛郎夫妇忍痛将老牛的皮剥下来,将牛的躯体埋于后山坡上。

织女和牛郎私订终身的事情,很快被天宫的玉皇大帝和圣母娘娘获悉。圣母娘娘勃然大怒,敕令天神下入凡间,将织女抓回天宫问罪。天神虽很同情织女,却也不敢违抗圣命。待牛郎外出不在家中之时,天神将织女抓回天界复命。牛郎回家后,见四处找寻不到织女的踪影,恍然已知是被天神抓去了。牛郎用老牛的皮制成鞋,用扁担挑着两个小孩,腾云驾雾,飞入云霄去追赶织女。眼见就要追上织女,圣母娘娘心中一急，遂拔下头上金簪,在银河上划了一道界限。本还是清澈见底的银河，霎时间浊浪排空,阻

Boy. From then on, the couple could only stare at each other from each side of the gap and shed tears. Finally, they got sympathy from the Queen Mother and she allowed them to meet once a year in the milky way on the seventh of July. It was said that on this night each year, millions of magpies would fly up from the human' s world to the milky way to build a bridge over the gap so that the Buffalo Boy and the Weaver Girl could have their precious reunion. Years and years later, a tradition formed. Single young girls will gather together to look up at the sky at night and look for the Altair and the Vega which is considered to be the Buffalo Boy and the Weaver Girl transformed, listening to the the lover' s whispers. The girls all wish to see the lover' s reunion and wish that they will be as clever as the fairy and their future husband could be well-content as the Buffalo Boy.

挡了牛郎追赶的步伐。从此以后，牛郎与织女夫妇只能天各一方。他们忠贞的爱情，终于得到了圣母娘娘的同情。圣母娘娘动了恻隐之心，遂准许他们每年七月初七在银河相会一次。传说每逢七月初七，人间的喜鹊就要飞入云霄，在银河为牛郎和织女搭鹊桥相会。后来人们相沿成习，在每逢七夕夜深人静之时，少女们都会聚集在一起仰望星空，寻找牛郎星与织女星，侧耳倾听牛郎与织女的悄悄话。少女们希望能亲眼目睹他们一年一度的相会盛况，乞求上天能让自己变成织女那样心灵手巧的人，祈祷自己能找到一位像牛郎一样称心如意的郎君。

Ⅱ. Customs

Customs about the festival are varied, such as *Qiqiao*, praying for kids, eating nuts, worshiping stars and sunbathing books and clothes.

Qiqiao

Since *Qiqiao* is a main activity of the Chinese Valentine's Day, it is also called *Qiqiao* Festival. On the night of the seventh day of the seventh lunar month every year, young girls will gather together in the courtyard and pray to the Vega for intelligence and skillfulness. Forms of celebrating *Qiqiao* vary in different parts of China, such as threading needles, spider netting, throwing needles and so on.

Celebrating the Birthday of the Old Cattle

On this day, children regularly go out to collect flowers and put them on the cattle's horn to celebrate the cattle's birthday. According to the folklore, Queen Mother created the milky way and stopped the couple from being together, and the cattle let his leather be flayed to help the Buffalo Boy to fly to Heaven to see his beloved wife. Thus, the custom of memorizing the old cattle's selfless dedication comes out.

二、习俗

民间有关七夕节的习俗有很多，主要有乞巧、种生求子、食巧果、拜魁星、晒衣书等。

乞巧

乞巧是七夕节的主要活动，民间又将七夕节称为乞巧节。乞巧，指的是在每年农历七月初七的夜晚，少女聚坐在庭院内向织女星乞求智巧。乞巧的形式有很多，如穿针乞巧、喜蛛应巧、投针验巧等。

为牛庆生

在七夕节的这一天，孩童们去郊外采摘野花，然后将野花挂在牛角上，名曰为牛庆祝生日。民间传说，圣母娘娘用银河将牛郎和织女分开。老牛为了帮助牛郎见到自己心爱的妻子织女，于是要牛郎将自己的皮剥下，以帮助牛郎飞入天宫。人们为了纪念老牛这种无私奉献的精神，于是便有了这一习俗。

Worshipping the Vega

Only girls can worship the Vega. The fairy's faith to love moves every young girl, which is why they gather together to worship her. On the Chinese's Valentine's Day, girls with their relatives and friends got together to worship the Vega. The ceremony is held mostly at night and it requires five to ten girls to attend. Under the magnificent moonlight, girls will put such sacrificial offerings as tea, wine, fruit on a table to worship the Vega. Besides, several bunches of flowers made by red paper will be put into a vase on both sides of the table. An incensory will be put in front of the vase. Girls who attend the worship have to abstain from meat and take a shower the previous day, then get together at a given time at a given place to worship the Vega. After the ceremony, girls will pray for a suitable husband while eating peanuts and melon seeds. Married women often wish to have a lovely baby soon.

拜祭织女

只有女子才能参加祭拜织女的活动。织女对爱情忠贞不渝的追求，感动了无数的少女。在七夕节的这一天，少女们相约自己要好的亲友，在一起共同祭拜织女。参加的人数是有所固定的，大多在五至十人之内，仪式一般在夜晚举行。姐妹们趁着美好的月色，在庭院内摆上供桌，然后置放茶、酒、水果等祭品。此外，还要在供桌的两旁，放上几朵鲜花，或用红纸扎成鲜花，将它们插入瓶内。在花瓶的前面，还要放置一个小香炉。相约拜祭的姐妹需要在前一日斋戒沐浴，然后在约定的时间和地点，共同参加祭拜。祭拜仪式结束后，人们一面吃花生、嗑瓜子，一面朝着织女星座，在心中默默祈祷，希望自己以后能嫁一位如意郎君。如果是已婚的妇女，则希望自己能早生贵子。

Eating *Qiaoguo*

The *Qiaoguo* is specially made for this day. The patterns and processes of making are varied. However, it is almost fried molasses. People mix heated sugar with flour and sesames, and place the mixture on a plate and wait till it dries, then slice it. Then the slices will be put into boiling oil to fry. Some ingenious girls can even make the slices into different shapes relevant to the Chinese Valentine's Day like birds or carved the melon into the shape of flowers and birds, and such kind of pattern is named *Huagua*.

Washing Hair

In many places of the Southern China, women like to wash their hair by the river on this day. It is said that dirt and sorrows can be washed away in this way. They arrange to wash hair together with the water, boiled cypress leaves and peach tree branches, by the river. This tradition is relevant to the worship of the holy water. It is believed that on that day, taking the water from a river is like taking the water from the milky way, which is called Vega's Holy Water. Girls will be blessed and

食巧果

巧果是七夕节特有的节庆食品。巧果有很多款式，制作的工艺也各不相同。但主要是油炸蜜糖。人们将糖浆与面粉、芝麻等物品搅拌在一起，然后将糖浆平摊在案板上，使其变成薄薄的一层。待糖浆冷却之后，将其再放入锅中油炸。心灵手巧的女子，还将糖浆制作成各种与七夕有关的花式图案，或将瓜果雕成奇花异鸟，或在瓜皮表面上浮雕图案。这种在瓜上雕刻图案，称为“花瓜”。

梳洗头发

妇女们在七夕节的这一天，喜欢去河边梳洗头发，以洗涤一年之中的污秽与烦恼。七夕之时，妇女们相约在一起去河边洗头，用柏树叶、桃树枝煎汤，然后梳洗头发。民间认为，七夕节这一天，倘若取泉水、河水，就如同取银河水一样。女子在这天沐浴头发，就被赋

protected by the Vega as long as they wash hair in this holy water.

予了特殊含义，表示用银河里的圣水净发，必可获得织女神的护佑。

Worshipping the Stars

This festival originally comes from people's worship of nature. Chinese ancient astrologists believed that there are seven groups of stars which stand for the directions in the sky, and they are called the Twenty-eight Constellations. Among them the brightest is called the Big Dipper, which can directly guide directions at night. The first star of the Big Dipper is called the Chief Star. As the Imperial Examinations popularized, the Number One Scholar was called Big Dipper of the Country, which

拜魁星

七夕源于人们对自然界的崇拜。中国古代的天文学认为，在东西南北各有七颗代表方位的星星，合称二十八星宿。其中以北斗星最为明亮，夜间可辨别方向。北斗星的第一颗星星，称之为魁星，又名"魁首"。科举考试兴起之后，中状元者被称为"魁元"，所以读书

means the best. From then on, July seventh is also called the Chief Star Festival by the scholars. People believe that July seventh is the birthday of the Chief Star, and that is why people who attend the Imperial Examinations all worship the Chief Star on July seventh, hoping that they would be the Number One Scholar and have a brilliant future.

Sunbathing Books and Clothes

It is a very popular activity to sunbath books and clothes on July seventh among people. This tradition started from a story which says that in ancient time people were used to sunbathing books on July seventh, and unlike others, a man named *Hao Long* went basking himself instead of sunbathing his books and clothes. People asked him why, he answered, "I am sunbathing books." Actually, he told others that he was sunbathing books as his way of showing off.

人又将七夕称为"魁星节"。民间认为,七月七日是魁星的生日。想求取功名的读书人特别崇拜魁星,于是在七月七日的这一天,他们都会祭拜魁星,以保佑自己能高中状元,官运亨通。

晒衣书

七月七日这一天,民间十分流行晒衣服和书籍。这一习俗源于民间传说,说是在古时七月七日这一天,人们有晒书的习俗。但是有个名叫郝隆的人,这天不去晒书,反而跑到太阳底下躺着晒太阳。别人问他,为何如此。他回答道:"我在晒书。"言下之意,晒肚皮就是晒书,以此夸耀自己满腹才学。

The *Zhongyuan* Festival
中元节

Zhongyuan Festival, also named as the Ghost Festival, *Yulanpen* Festival or the Mid-July Day, is a traditional festival celebrated by the Chinese to make sacrifice to their ancestors. It is on July 15th in the lunar calendar. The *Zhongyuan* Festival is similar to the Halloween and it's a day to make sacrifice to the ancestors and pray for peace.

中元节，又名“鬼节”、“盂兰盆节”、“七月半”，即每年农历的七月十五日，是中国人祭祀祖先的传统节日。中元节与西方的万圣节相似，主要是为了祭祀亡灵、祈祷平安。

Ⅰ. Origin

The *Zhongyuan* Festival originates from Taoism. It is considered by Taoism that the Three *Yuans*, which are heaven, earth and water, are the basis to build up everything. The heaven and the earth are the foundation of the universe, and water is the origin of life. Correspondingly, the Heaven *Guan*, Earth *Guan*, Water *Guan* are established. The Taoists call the 15th day of the 1st, 7th and 10th lunar month respectively as *Shangyuan*, *Zhongyuan* and *Xiayuan* in memory of the Three *Guans*. Blessing ceremonies is usually performed on

一、来历

中元节的说法源于道教。道教认为“天、地、水”是构成万物的基本，谓之“三元”。天地是宇宙万物的根本，水是生命的起源，与之对应的又有“天官、地官、水官”。为了纪念“三官”，道教分别将正月十五日称为“上元”，七月十五日称为“中元”，十月十五日称为“下元”。正月十五日

the *Shangyuan* Festival, also well known as Lantern Festival, which occurs on the 15th day of the 1st lunar month. The 15th day of the 7th lunar month called *Zhongyuan* Festival or Ghost Festival is made to forgive the sins of the dead. The *Xiayuan* Festival, on the 15th day of the 10th lunar month, is an occasion to help people release themselves from misfortune, or to make confessions for sinners. Dozens of grand religious ceremonies are held on *Zhongyuan* Festival to pray for favorable weather, a prosperous and peaceful country. There was a legend in Taoism telling the origin of the Three *Yuans*. A man named *Chen Zidao* married the daughter of the Dragon King. After the marriage, the king' s daughter gave birth to three boys named the Heaven *Guan*, Earth *Guan*, Water *Guan* respectively on the 15th day of the 1st, 7th, and 10th lunar month. With special skills and infinite power, the three brothers were granted the title of the Great Three *Yuans* by the Emperor of Heaven. Power of blessing, pardoning and disaster dispelling were granted respectively to them. Three *Yuans* Palace or Three *Guan*' s Temple was built in memory of them. Therefore, *Zhongyuan* Festival turned out to be an important day for making sacrifice to ancestors.

Zhongyuan Festival is also named *Yulan*-

谓之“上元节”，即元宵节，主要举行赐福仪式。七月十五日谓之“中元节”，即“鬼节”，主要是赦免亡灵的罪孽。十月十五日谓之“下元节”，主要为了解脱人们的厄运，或为世间有罪过的人忏悔。中元节的这一天，人们要举行隆重的宗教仪式，以祈祷风调雨顺、国泰民安。有关“三元”的来历，道教有一个传说。相传有个名叫陈子祷的人，他与龙王的女儿喜结连理。婚后，龙王的女儿怀有身孕，分别于正月十五日、七月十五日、十月十五日诞下了天官、地官、水官三兄弟。三兄弟身怀绝技，各个神通广大，拥有无穷的法力。天帝神君赐封他三人为神仙，谓之“三元大帝”，分别掌管人间的赐福、赦罪、解厄三事。人们为了祭祀他们，建造有“三元宫”或“三官庙”。中元节便成为重要的祭祖之日。

中元节还有一种说

pen Festival. The word *Yulan* derives from the Sanskrit with the meaning of suspend, which means someone be hung down. And *Pen* is a ware for collecting worshipping gifts in Buddhism. It comes from a Buddhist story called *How Mulian saved his mother*. There is a legend that *Mulian*, one of the disciples of Sakyamuni, applied himself closely to the study of Buddhism and gained infinite power finally. He noticed with his miraculous eyes that his mother was suffering great pains in the hell. Thinking of the love and care from his mother in his childhood, the kindhearted and filial man tried to feed his mother with bowls of rice. However, rice was turned to dust the moment it reached his mother's hand. He could not do anything despite his magic power, he turned to Buddha for help. And he was told that only with the strength of all the monks could his mother be free from pain since she was deeply sinned in her previous life. The Buddha instructed *Mulian* that he needed to get the *Yulanpen* tributes well prepared and treat the monks from different places respectfully with all kinds of food on July 15th, the time that all monks finished their praying, so that his mother could be saved. *Mulian* performed what Buddha had told him and finally he succeeded in saving his mother. Thus, the

法，名叫"盂兰盆节"。"盂兰"源于梵语，意为"倒悬"，即人被倒挂、悬吊。盆，指的是佛教中装有供品的器皿。盂兰盆节起源于佛教中"目连救母"的故事。传说在释迦牟尼的众多弟子之中，有一位名叫目连的僧人。他苦习佛法，终得正果，拥有无穷的法术。他是一个至善至孝之人，为了报答父母的养育之恩，他用自己的神眼，观察到自己的母亲在幽冥地界所遭受的痛苦。目连痛彻心扉，于是用钵盛饭给自己的母亲食用。但是饭食刚送到母亲的手中，尚未入口便化为灰烬。目连虽有神力，却也束手无策。他恳请佛祖帮助他，佛祖说："你母亲前世罪孽深重，你一个人是无法解救的，你要依靠十方僧众的道力才行。"佛祖教导目连，要在七月十五日众僧修行圆满之日，毕恭毕敬摆设盛大的盂兰盆供品，用百味饮食供

deed is followed by people every July 15th. Elaborate meals will be provided to the poor. Buddhist scripture will be recited to release the souls of the dead from purgatory.

养十方众僧，只有这样才能解救目连的母亲。目连按照佛祖的教导，果真解救了自己的母亲。此后，人们纷纷效仿目连，在七月十五这一天做“盂兰盆会”，诵念经书，给贫苦之人施舍食物，求佛法超度死去的亡灵。

Zhongyuan Festival is regarded as Ghost Day in Chinese folklore. It is said that, ghosts and spirits, with the permission of the king of Hell, would come out to watch the good and evil of the people alive on July 1st. They are believed to visit their own former houses, enjoying the ritualistic food offerings and fetching paper money burned by their family. And July 15th is the deadline on which all departed ghosts had to go back to hell since the door between our world and hell would be closed, otherwise, they would be abandoned. On this day, water lanterns are floated along the river by people to direct the ghosts back to another world.

“鬼节”是民间对中元节的说法。相传在七月初一的那一天，幽冥地界的总管阎罗王就要打开鬼门关，让大大小小的鬼魂来到人间，去观察世间之人是为善，还是为恶。鬼魂还会在这几日前往自己的家中，领取亲人们烧给他们的纸钱，以及享用供品。七月十五日是幽冥地界关闭大门之日，所有在外游荡的鬼魂都必须返回阴间，否则就会成为孤魂野鬼。七月十五日这一天，人们在水边放河灯，意在给鬼魂指引回家的道路。

Ⅱ. Customs

There are many customs about *Yulanpen* Festival, such as ancestors' worship, lanterns lighting, grappling with ghosts (*Qianggu*), playing the drama of *Zhong Kui* and holding the *Yulanpen* ceremony, etc..

Ancestors' Worship

The ancestors' worship on the 15th day of the 7th lunar calendar is commonly called Mid-July Day ancestors' worship. It is the very day of summer falling into autumn. The hot summer is over and the cool autumn is just around the corner. The deceased ancestors are believed to go back home to see the descendants, thus, ritualistic offerings, spirit paper money will be offered. Rituals are different from region to region, however, they are generally performing on July 15th. A saying named three days before and four days after means that paper money can be burnt and the ritualistic food offerings can be prepared three days before or four days after *Zhongyuan* Festival which is very popular in many areas. According to the multifarious rituals, ancestral tablets could never be moved while worshipping. Usually, they could only be moved one by one and put respectfully on the alter for sacrifice on July 15th. Then the incense is burnt in front of each tablet to worship ances-

二、习俗

民间有关中元节的节日习俗有很多，主要有祭祖、放河灯、抢孤、演钟馗戏、举办盂兰盆会等。

祭祖

农历七月十五日的祭祖，民间俗称“七月半”祭祖。按照中国的传统历法，这一天正好处于夏秋交替之际。酷热的夏天刚刚过去，凉爽的秋天就要来临。人们相信祖先会在这个时候返回自己的家中探望子孙，所以后辈们需准备供品与冥钱祭祀祖先。各地祭拜的仪式多有不同，大抵都在七月十五日的这一天举行。不少地方的人们还流行“前三后四”的说法，即中元节的前三天或后四天，都可以烧冥钱、摆供品，以祭奠已逝亲人的亡灵。祭拜的仪式也比较繁芜。在平常的日子里，如果需要祭拜的话，祖先的灵位是不能移动的。只有

tors. Three meals are served every morning, noon and evening till the end of the *Zhongyuan* Festival. A portrait of the deceased will be taken out and hung in the hall if there is one. The family members kneel down to worship ancestors in turns according to their ranks in the family hierarchy. What happened in the last year must be reported to ancestors by the elders together with the rest of the family members, and then the elders beg an ancestors to pray for the families' peace and happiness.

Eating soybeans has been prevailing in *Jiangsu* and *Zhejiang* provinces while worshipping. It's the season to harvest the soybean at the time, and the whole family gather together to talk about the past events while eating soybeans boiled in salty water after the ceremony. In memory of a general named *Li Daiwen* in the late *Ming* Dynasty, drinking soybean milk is very popular for Shanghainese on the 14th day of the 7th lunar month, the day before the *Zhongyuan* Festival. It is said that it's very

到七月半祭祖的这一天，后辈才将先人的牌位一一请出来，毕恭毕敬地放在专门做祭拜用的供桌上。然后在每一位先人的牌位前插上香，每日清晨、中午、黄昏分别供奉三次茶饭，直到中元节结束为止。倘若家中有先人的遗像，还需将先人的遗像或照片请出来，挂在厅堂里。祭拜的时候，按照辈分和长幼次序，给每位先人磕头，然后由家中年长的人带领子孙默默祷告，向先人汇报家中这一年来发生的大小事情，祈求先人保佑全家人平安幸福。

在江浙一带，人们在祭祖的时候还特别流行吃毛豆。那时，正是毛豆成熟的季节，用盐水煮上一大盆，祭奠完祖先以后，一家人围坐在一起，一边吃毛豆，一边述说过去的往事。在中元节的前一天，即农历七月十四日，上海人还流行喝豆浆。相传，这是为了纪念

critical that the *Qing* army invaded *Shanghai* in the south in the late *Ming* Dynasty. *Li Dai-wen's* army held such a strong defence that the city could not be taken over easily. It was then surrounded by the *Qing* army, and the water and food supply had been cut off. People donated all food to the defending troops. However, all food was exhausted a month later. On July 14th, General *Li*' s birthday, he milled the rest of soybean in his house into soybean milk to feed the hungry soldiers , which encouraged them a lot. Knowing that there was no food in the city for several days, the *Qing* army began to attack the city heavily. *Li* told the remaining troops to break through the encirclement, when he returned to his house and bravely gave his life for his country by killing himself, leaving a note to the *Qing* army, hoping that they would take good care of the innocent citizens of *Shanghai* instead of killing them. Later, a grand City God Temple worshipping General *Li* was built and he was honored as God of *Shanghai*. Soybeans are made into soybean milk by people in *Shanghai* on *Li*' s birthday, every 14th of the lunar July, to memorize this beloved leader who sacrificed his life for the country.

明朝末年一位名叫李待问的将军。明朝末年，清军南下攻入上海城内，形势十分危急。李待问带领抗清的义军，固守上海。当时上海的城防工事十分坚固，清军一时间难以攻入。于是便采取围城的策略，断绝了城内的粮食供给，城内的守军早已粮草断绝。百姓们十分拥戴义军，纷纷将家中的粮食献出来给义军。又过去了一个月，百姓家中的粮食也断绝了。七月十四日原本是李将军的生辰，为了犒劳前方的将士，他将家中仅有的几斗黄豆献出来，磨成豆浆，分发给前方的战士们充饥，鼓舞了义军的斗志。这时，清兵的将领得知城内早已断粮好几日了，便大举攻入城内。李将军嘱咐残余的义军冲出重围，自己则返回府中，在案桌上立下遗书，希望清兵攻入城内后不要滥杀无辜，应爱护上海无辜百姓，遂自刎殉

Lantern Floating

The *Zhongyuan* Festival was celebrating the dead. So the lanterns could only be floated on water to worship the deceased. One of local folk tales is that the lantern floating is a religious ceremony started in temples for the purpose of transmuting and absolving the sufferings of ghosts. Later, people commemorated the deceased through floating lanterns as the custom became popular. The designs of lanterns are varied, and the most common style is the lotus lantern, and there are also

国。后来,上海的百姓为了祭奠李将军,在城内建造了雄伟的城隍庙,并尊奉李将军为上海的城隍。每年农历七月十四日,即李将军的生辰之日,上海的百姓就磨黄豆、喝豆浆,以缅怀这位受百姓爱戴、为国捐躯的将领。

放河灯

中元节是给阴间亡故之人庆祝的,因而只能在水中张灯,于是便有了放河灯的习俗。关于放河灯有不少地方传说,放河灯最早是一种兴起于寺院的宗教祭祀活动,目的在于超度孤魂野鬼。后来这种习俗传入民间,人们便以放河灯的形式,追思亡魂,祭奠亡故之人。河灯的样式较多,有白菜灯、西瓜灯、莲花灯等,尤以莲花灯最为普遍。河灯的制作工艺各有不同,首先需购买大张的彩纸,然后将大红、浅红、黄、绿、紫五种彩纸裁成大小一致的方块,再折成中间方

cabbage and watermelon lanterns. One of the lanterns' making processes shows that one should prepare many large pieces of colored-paper at first, then cut bright red, pale red, yellow, green, purple paper into square pieces of the same size, and fold them into square supporting paper ,after that, stretch the four corners out, then a lotus lantern is made. The paper lantern's bottom should be put into pine oil for a while and dry it in the yard to reinforce the shape and make it waterproof. After finishing the lanterns, people float water lanterns along the river while taoists or monks playing folk tunes with the mouth-organ (*Sheng*) and panpipe (*Xiao*).

形的托底，然后将四角伸出来，便制成了莲花灯。扎好灯后需浸油，先将松香放入锅中烧熔，再将扎好的纸灯的灯底在松油里浸一下。把它放在院子里晾干，底子上的油就凝固住了，可以起到固定形状与防止浸水的作用。制作完毕后，由道士或者和尚用笙箫吹奏民间小调，在沿河的岸边做起法事，然后众人在河边放河灯。

Burning *Baoyi*

Baoyi, also called *Baofu*, is a paper bag containing paper money for the ghosts in fact. A folklore holds the idea that the new deceased spirits will visit home from the 1st to 7th of the Ghost Month, July, and the old deceased who passed away over three years will be back home from the 8th to 15th of the month. When the mid-July is approaching, the families begin to prepare *Wangsheng* Money, i.e.the Joss Paper we know. Usually the housewives go to the Buddhist or Taoist temple to purchase the ghost money and write on the bag "to the honorable dead mother or father

烧包衣

包衣，又名"包袱"，实际就是装有冥钱的纸袋。民间认为七月是鬼月，新亡故者初一至初七要返回家中探亲，倘若是已故达三年以上的老亡故者，则要在初八至十五返回家中探亲。每当七月十五快来临之际，家人则开始留心准备往生钱，即冥钱。一般由家中的主妇前往附近的佛寺或道观中购买，然后在买来的包

× × ×" and with one's name signed next to it. One will write a Chinese Character seal on the seal of the bag after writing. Getting rice, fish, meat and tofu well prepared, a housewife closes the door, puts all bowls and chopsticks on the table of the hall and transfers rice to a bowl one noon from July 12th to the 15th. The master of the house burns paper bags in front of the shrine and pay homage, and hopes that ancestors will bless them. The unmarried son and daughter should also kowtow. Then setting off firecrackers, the whole family will have a meal together.

袱上书写"已故先妣（考）某某大人收"，旁边落款署上各自姓名。包袱写好后，在封口处写上"封"字。从七月十二日至十五日，主妇在某一天的中午备好饭、菜、鱼、肉和豆腐，然后关闭大门，在堂屋的大桌上摆上碗筷，将新鲜的米饭添入碗中。男主人则在神龛前烧包袱，一边烧一边祈祷祖宗保佑，烧完叩拜。未出嫁的女儿与未婚的儿子，也需要一起叩拜，然后鸣放鞭炮，全家吃饭。

Yulanpen Festival

Yulanpen Festival, a grand festival of Buddhism, is named from the tale how *Mulian* saved his mother. The festival originally means showing gratitude for parents' fostering. The custom spreads to China by a knowledgeable monk from India in West *Jin* Dynasty. Deceased parents' souls are released from sufferings through reciting Buddhist scriptures and per-

盂兰盆会

盂兰盆会是佛教的盛大节日，因目连救母的故事而得名，其初衷旨在感恩父母的养育之恩。西晋时期，天竺的得道高僧来到中原，将这一习俗传至中国。通过诵经做

forming rites, which matches to the Confucian sense of piety so as to be advocated by emperors in all dynasties. During the period of *Liang Wudi* of the Southern Dynasty, *Yulanpen* Dharma Assembly was held every year, repaying kindness from ancestors and hoping for an everlasting country. It becomes so prevalent that *Yulanpen* Festivals were held by both nobilities and common people for their well-beings.

法事，为亡故的双亲超度功德，这与中国儒家学说中的"孝道"伦理传统相一致，颇受历代帝王的尊崇。南朝梁武帝时期，每年都会举办大型的盂兰盆法会，以报答祖先的恩德，祈求江山永固。唐代以后，佛教的法会更为流行，上至帝王诸侯，下至平民百姓，纷纷举行各种形式的盂兰盆会，以祈求安康。

Qianggu

Qianggu (grappling with ghosts) is a custom that is peculiar to people living in south *Fujian* on *Zhongyuan* Festival. On that day, people put offerings or a flag on the top of a tall column with grease on its surface. Many people will climb the column together to compete to take the offerings or flag. The one who gets the offerings or flags is the winner. As the winner will not only be awarded with a trophy, but also get blessings from the spirits.

抢孤

抢孤是福建闽南特有的中元节习俗。中元节那一天，人们将供品或旗子放置于高柱之上，将柱子涂满油脂，令众人同爬其柱，先得旗、物者胜出。参加者不但能取得奖品，且代表自己会得到神鬼的祝福。

Nadam Fair
那达慕大会

The Nadam Fair is a traditional festival held once a year for people of Mongolian Nationality. Grand celebrations take place between July and August of the lunar calendar every year. On that day, people from all directions have their best suits on to participate in, or appreciate the competitions.The Nadam means recreation or games in Mongolian. It is not only a grand celebration, but also a good physical exercise for Mongolians.

那达慕大会是蒙古族人民一年一度的传统节日，于每年农历的七八月间举行盛大的庆祝活动。在那一天，四面八方的人们穿着节日的盛装，纷纷前来参赛或观赏比赛。“那达慕”是蒙古语，其意为“娱乐”、“游戏”。那达慕不仅是蒙古人的一项庆祝盛会，也是蒙古人深为喜爱的一项体育活动。

Ⅰ. Origin

One story which tells the origin of the Nadam Fair starting from *Han* Dynasty says that the ancient Mongolians have had the religious practice of offering sacrifices to *Aobao*. The so-called *Aobao* are actually piles of stones. Stones are usually piled into a solid pagoda in which images of deities are enshrined. In addition a long pole decorated with

一、来历

关于那达慕的起源有这样一个传说。古代的蒙古族人有着“祭敖包”的宗教习俗，它最早开始于汉代，历史十分久远。所谓敖包即“石堆”。蒙古人一般选择一个景色宜人、开阔的高地，用石

cloth strips of scripture or horns, or wool of livestocks is put on it. The location of the stone pagoda is chosen on an open highland with a pleasant outlook. The Mongolian people gather around the *Aobao* and hold sacrifice activities to show thanks to nature for bringing them up. During the time of Genghis Khan, the Mongolian people had held Nadam rituals. With the military victory in West Asia, Genghis Khan held grand Nadam celebrations with his armies on their way back home. Afterwards, the ceremony has become the most important festival for Mongolians.

头堆砌成一座圆形的实心宝塔，里面供放着神像，顶端还需竖立着饰有经文布条或牲畜毛角的长杆。蒙古族人民聚集在敖包周围，举行祭祀活动，以感谢大自然的哺育之恩。在成吉思汗时代，蒙古人就要举行那达慕仪式。成吉思汗在西亚取得了军事上的胜利，在率军凯旋的路途上，举行了盛大的那达慕庆祝仪式。后来，这一仪式逐渐发展为蒙古人重要的节日。

II. Customs

At first, three basic activities were held in the Nadam Fair. Wrestling, archery, horse racing, were regarded as the three skills which men should shall master. Afterwards, the activities such as throwing, polo, etc. have been added to make the occasion grander.

二、习俗

起初的时候，那达慕大会主要举办三项活动，即摔跤、射箭、赛马，被称为男子汉应当具备的三种技艺。后来，那达慕所举办的活动项目有所发展，增加了投掷、马球等项目，场面盛大。

Wrestling

Wrestling is a popular game for Mongolian people, and it's also the most attractive one in Nadam Fair. Wrestling is called *Pok*,

摔跤

摔跤是蒙古族人十分喜爱的一项体育活动，也是那达慕大会上最引人注

and the wrestler is called *Pokqing* in Mongolian. Wrestlers need to play in a specially-made ethnic wrestling costume with dragon or bird patterns and so on in upper clothing, and wide drapes made of silk fabric in lower clothing with five-color pattern embroidered near knees, and wide leather belt or silk belt around the waist.

Mongolian wrestling is mainly featured as follows: The wrestlers are not limited in region and weight. Only one round will determine the winner. The number of participants of wrestling must be an even number, for example, four, eight, and sixteen, etc.. Before the game, a noble and prestiged senior will be selected to match the competitors. After chanting the anthem of wrestlers by people, the wrestlers will wave their hands for greetings, and dance hawk dance into the competition field. Both sides of the wrestlers will salute to the chairpersons' platform, and then turn around clockwise. Then they will wait for the order from the referee to begin the game. Both

目的节目。摔跤在蒙语中称"博克",摔跤手在蒙古语中则叫"博克庆"。摔跤手需要穿着一种特制的民族摔跤服,上饰有精美的龙形、鸟形等图案,下着绸料制成的套裤,多宽大有褶皱,双膝处有绣制五彩图案,腰缠宽皮带或绸带。

蒙式摔跤的特点主要有:摔跤手的人选不受地域和体重的限制,一跤定胜负。参赛的选手需为2的倍数,如4、8、16等。比赛开始前,需推选出一位德高望重的长者对参赛选手进行比赛的配对。然后等人们咏唱完摔跤手歌后,摔跤手挥手致意,并且需跳着老鹰舞进入场地。摔跤手双方向主席台行礼,并顺时针转一圈,再由裁判员发令,宣布比赛开始,双方再握手致意,

sides will shake hands to greet each other before the game begins. Although there are over one hundred wrestling ways, the main principles are almost the same which originates from thirteen basic ways. The biggest feature of Mongolian wrestling is that the players can't hold the competitor's legs. In addition, hitting the face, kicking the belly, and pulling hair of competitors, etc., are forbidden, too.

The reward for the wrestling champion is a sheep or several tea bricks, and the reward for the champion of a relatively grand competition is a horse fully equipped with saddles. If the wrestler obtains the champion in league-scaled competition, he will have the right to wear *Zhangga*, which is a necklace decorated with five-color silk. To wear *Zhangga* is a dream for many wrestlers.

正式开摔。摔跤的技巧颇多，甚至达到了一百多种技巧，可万变不离其宗，主要是由十三个基本技巧变幻而来。蒙古式摔跤最大的特点，就是不能抱对手的腿部，其余规则还包括不准打脸、踢肚子、拉头发等。

摔跤冠军一般获得的奖励是一头羊或者是几块砖茶，而较大型的比赛奖励则是一匹装好了全套鞍的马。如果在全盟参加的摔跤手比赛中拿到了冠军，即可享有佩带"章嘎"的荣誉。章嘎是一种五色绸条做成的项圈，能够佩带上章嘎是许多摔跤手梦寐以求的。

Archery

Mongolian people have been living a nomadic and hunting life for a long time with the bows and arrows as the necessities. During their leisure time, bows and arrows are regarded as their daily entertainment tools, so the archery competition exists for long. At present, archery is a kind of competitive sport to practice the arm muscle and eyesight. Mongo-

射箭

蒙古族长久以来都过着游牧狩猎的生活，弓箭是生存的必需品。闲暇之余，日常生活所需的弓箭成为娱乐的工具，射箭比赛也由来已久。如今，射箭是一项增强臂力、锻炼目力的体育竞技项目。

lian archery competition mainly consists of two types, still archery and riding archery. Still archery refers to shoot a target wrapped with a leather bag which is one meter wide and two meters long. The target is a stump erected in forty or fifty meters far from the shooting place. The competitors are divided into groups and supposed to compete at the shooting place. The competition ranks are determined by the times of the shooting target. Several persons can hold an extemporaneous competition due to its flexibility and convenience. Riding archery is generally held in big fairs or joyful celebrations. The shooters are supposed to shoot the target while riding along the athletic track which is usually eighty-five meters long and four meters wide. There are three targets set along the track, and every other target is twenty-five meters.

The traditional bow is generally made of wood with ox horns set at both ends of it. The back of the bow is semi-circle, and the middle part is developing into a round handle with cowheels stretched tightly as the bowstring. The arrow is about one meter long with vari-

蒙古族的射箭比赛主要分为两种，静射和骑射。静射是在距离射击处四五十米远处竖立一个木桩，然后裹着皮袋为靶，宽1米，长2米。参赛者可分为小组，在固定地点轮流立射，以中靶多少决定名次。由于这种比赛灵活方便，几个人聚集一处，即可即兴演练。骑射一般在大的集会或喜庆节日举行，射手骑马持弓箭沿跑道边跑、边射。跑道通常为85米长、4米宽，沿跑道设3个靶位，每个靶位相距25米。

传统的弓一般为木质，两端镶嵌有牛角；弓背为半圆形，中间渐内收成圆握柄，绷以牛筋弓弦。箭长约100厘米左右，箭镰形状多样，多为

ous arrow sickles which are usually made of iron or bone. Sometimes, the end of the arrow shaft is decorated with three rows of hawk feathers.

铁质，亦有骨质，箭杆尾饰三排鹰羽。

Horse Racing

Since ancient times, the Mongolian people are entitled to heroic people on horseback, Mongolian people chase for skillful archery as well as extreme riding skill as their top goal. There is a great variety of horse racing in Mongolian Nationality, mainly including walking a horse, running a horse, and racing a horse for a variety show. Racing a horse is usually held on the plain and open grassland with scores of competitors racing together at the same time, and the ranks will be determined by the orders which the participants run to the destination without considering the time.

赛马

蒙古族自古以来就有"马上民族"的美称，蒙古族人不仅追求箭术纯熟，也以马术卓绝为最高目标。蒙古族的赛马种类繁多，主要有走马赛、奔马赛和花样赛。赛马常在平坦开阔的草原上进行，几十名赛手不分组，同时起跑，不计时间，以到达目的地的先后次序决定名次。当然，需按照指定的路线赛马，并要返

Certainly, the racing route is set in advance, and the competitors are supposed to return to the starting line. Usually, the informal racing horse isn't equipped with saddles in order to reduce the load of the racing horse, and to protect the competitors from being heavily injured in case they fall down from the racing horse. Moreover, the competitors do not have to wear riding boots, but they are fond of wearing a colorful robe and a green kerchief on head, which makes the competitors attractive as well as bright and brave.

回起跑地。民间的赛马多不备马鞍，一为减轻马的负荷，二为防范赛手跌下来时不致有太大伤害。选手也不穿马靴，但他们喜欢穿着彩袍，头上裹着绿巾，不仅扎眼醒目，更显英姿飒爽。

The racing events include running a horse and walking a horse. Running a horse is the most attractive event in Nadam Fair with dozens to hundreds of competitors of all ages. The competitors are usually young players. The youngest competitor is only seven or eight years old, and generally speaking, they are almost twelve or thirteen years old. Running a horse, as its name implying, stresses on the running speed of the racing horses, so only the straight racing track can purely reflect the speed of running horses. The racing tracks are divided into groups of twenty kilometers, thirty kilometers, and forty kilometers, and the winner is the first to reach the destination.

赛马的项目包括快马赛和走马赛。快马赛是那达慕大会上最引人注目的活动。参加者少则数十，多则上百，参赛选手年龄不限，大都是少年，其中年龄最小者只有七八岁，一般不过十二三岁。快马赛，赛如其名，讲究的就是马的速度，故以直线赛程方能纯粹地体现赛马的飞速。赛程有20、30、40公里几种类别，以先到达终点者为胜。

Walking a horse competes against the firmness and lightness of racing horses' steps.

走马赛，主要是比赛马步伐的稳健与轻快。参

Most of the competitors are adults, and walking a horse is especially focusing on skills. But the number of horse participating in the competition is not limited generally.

加走马赛的一般是成年人，特别讲究技巧，参赛的马匹数一般不受限制。

Throwing

Mongolian people are enthusiastic about a game entitled as throwing. The object to be thrown is like a short handle sickle. The players are supposed to throw in a distance or at a certain target with a sickle-like wood wrapped up with sheetmetal like lead, copper, or iron, etc.. The throwing object for competition is usually five hundred grams and sometimes the weight is not definite. And the throwing place for competition is usually a plain rectangular playground of seven hundred and fifty meters. A throwing line is underlined at one end of the ground and the throwing objects are three round stakes of fifty centimeters high at the other end. Every competitor can throw three times each time within thirty seconds in competition. Any throwing posture is allowed. Scoring for throwing is described as the following: Three shots is ten points, two shots is six points and one shot two. The full score is thirty for three throwings, and the ranks are decided by scores which player gets.

投掷

蒙古人十分热衷玩一种名为投掷的游戏。投掷的物品，形状像一把短柄的镰刀。投掷即用铅、铜或铁等金属片，包扎在一根形似镰刀的木头上，然后向远处掷去或者掷准某一处。比赛时，投掷的重量通常为 500 克，当然有的时候也没有明确的规定。比赛场地一般选在长度为 750 米左右的长方形平坦地上。在场地一端画一条投掷线，投掷目标为圆形木柱 3 根，柱高 50 厘米。正式比赛时，每人以 3 次为限，每次投掷时间不超过 30 秒。姿势不限，计分方法如下：击中 3 根木柱为 10 分，击中两根为 6 分，击中一根为 2 分。投掷 3 次，满分为 30 分，按总分多少排名次。

Polo

Polo is popular by Mongolians. Both of the players on two sides will participate in the competition with T-shape sticks in their hands. While the horse chasing each other, the players shot the ball at the goal, which is fierce, exciting and interesting. The official polo game lasts only eight minutes every round. At break, it is necessary to change the horses, otherwise both athletes and horses cannot tolerate the exercise strength. And the demand for polo exercise is strict in horses, riding skills and fields.

马球

马球是一项受蒙古族人欢迎的体育运动项目。参加比赛的双方队员手持T形拐棒，骑在马上击球射门，纵马互相追逐，比赛场面既紧张激烈，又饶有风趣。马球的正式比赛，每局仅有8分钟，一局间休息时要更换马匹，因为这项运动无论运动员还是马匹，运动的负荷都非常大。马球运动对马匹、骑术和场地要求都很高。

The Mid-Autumn Festival
中秋节

Mid-Autumn Festival, also known as Mid-August or Moon Festival, is celebrated on the 15th day of the 8th lunar month. The full moon on that day is a symbol of reunion, therefore, it is called *Tuanyuan* Festival in China. The Mid-Autumn Festival is another important festival after the Spring Festival, Tomb-sweeping Festival, and Dragon Boat Festival. It is a traditional festival for a family reunion and enjoying a chat.

中秋节，又名“八月半”、“月亮节”，即农历的八月十五日。因为这一天月亮满圆，象征团圆，又称为“团圆节”。中秋节是继春节、清明节、端午节之后又一个重要的节日。中秋节是阖家团聚、共叙亲情的传统佳节。

Ⅰ. Origin

There are nearly three legends about the origin of the Mid-Autumn Festival: The first one tells that it originates from the ancient people's worship to the moon, the second one shows that it come from the custom of seeking ideal mate under the moon, and the third one explains that it has its roots in the custom of offering sacrifices to the god of earth by ancient people in autumn. The Mid-Autumn Festival became a festival in the *Tang* Dynasty

一、来历

中秋节的起源，大致有三种说法：一是源于古人对月亮的崇拜，二是源于月下觅偶的习俗，三是古人有秋天祭拜土地神的习俗。中秋节演变为节日，则源自于唐代。唐代将中秋节称为“端正月”，在民间还举行各种节庆活动，此后渐成惯

when it was called *Duanzheng* Month and all sorts of festival activities were held. Gradually it became a convention. It became the official legal festival after the *Song* Dynasty and turned increasingly important in the *Ming* and *Qing* dynasties. Then it could be equaled to other traditional festivals such as the New Year' s Day, and it became one of the important festivals in China.

例。宋代以后，中秋节成为官方的法定节日。明清时期，中秋节的地位越来越重要，与元旦等传统节日并驾齐驱，成为中国重要的节日之一。

Ⅱ. Customs

Various activities will be held on that day such as moon sacrifice, moon appreciating, eating mooncakes, sending melons, etc.. In southern areas of *Fujian* Province, one special activity called Mooncake Gambling is prevalent.

二、习俗

中秋节这一天要举办各类活动，诸如祭月、赏月、吃月饼、送瓜等。在福建省的南部地区，还流行着一种十分特别的庆祝活动，即“中秋博饼”。

Moon Sacrifice

As the oldest festival activity of the Mid-Autumn Festival, the moon sacrifice is associated with the sacrifice in ancient times. The moon, or *Chang'e* we are familiar with, was considered the goddess of the moon among the people. Sacrifice activities were held in spring as well as autumn. The autumn sacrifice was for people to express their thanks to the god of earth and pray for an abundant harvest of all crops in the harvest season of mid-autumn. Meanwhile, the goddess of the

祭月

祭月是中秋节最古老的节日活动，它与远古先民的祭祀有关。民间将月亮视为神仙，称之为“月神”。“月神”就是我们熟知的嫦娥。中国人不仅在春天举行祭祀活动，就是在秋天也举行祭祀。所谓秋祀，指的是每当秋季中旬这一收获时节，人们需要拜谢土地神，以祈

moon needed to be worshiped, too. The ancients believed crops were granted with dew by the moon. Moreover, farming time was made according to the wax and wane of the moon.

The ceremony of moon sacrifice usually takes place at night in Mid-Autumn. During the ceremony, men and women will burn incense and pray in respectful silence. The way to express the gratitude varies in different regions, but most of them kneel down towards the orientation where moon rises. Melons and fruits will be prepared as offerings which are pears, apples, grapes, watermelons, etc. on altar table in northern China and grapefruits, taros, bananas, persimmons, peanuts and lotus roots in Southern China. As the moon rises slowly above the horizon, people burn the first piece of incence. Women worship first, and then the children follows, mumbling. After the ceremony, the altar table will be taken away, and offerings will be distributed to the people who do the worshipping.

Moon Appreciating

It is a popular activity to appreciate the moon on Mid-Autumn Festival. People had a tradition of steering a boat on the river and enjoyed the beautiful moonlight as early as the *Jin* Dynasty. Emperor *Xuanzong* of Tang and

祷五谷丰登。不过，秋祀还需要拜谢月神。古人认为月亮不仅赐予露水于五谷，而且依照月亮的圆缺能计算出农耕的时间。

祭祀月亮的仪式一般在中秋夜晚。祭祀时，男女都要面容整肃，烧香祭拜。各地的拜谢方式有所不同，但大多需朝月亮出来的方向跪拜。人们在朝拜时，需要摆设各类瓜果作为供品。北方的供案上，多摆放梨、苹果、葡萄、西瓜等瓜果。南方的供案上，多摆放柚子、芋头、香蕉、柿子、花生、藕等蔬菜与瓜果。待月亮缓缓升起，即烧起头香，妇女先拜，孩童次之。人们在祭拜时，口中还念念有词。祭拜完后，人们要撤掉供案，所供之品也给祭拜者分食。

赏月

赏月是一种普遍的中秋活动。晋代之时，人们就有泛舟江上，欣赏月色的习俗。唐玄宗与杨贵妃在中秋之夜驾临太液

Yang Yuhuan paid their visit to *Taiye Chi* and enjoyed the full moon on the night of the Mid-Autumn Festival. On the night of the Mid-Autumn Festival in Southern *Song* Dynasty, people from wealthy families posed themselves up and gathered together to enjoy the beautiful moonlight in pavilions, balustrades and rockeries. While ordinary people rushed to the restaurants to appreciate the moon. Children were larking about all night, and the night market was bedlam all night long. During the *Qing* Dynasty, there was a prevalent activity known as walking the moon. On that night, women dressed up themselves formally and went out with friends. They didn't stop walking until the cock crew at dawn.

池以望月。南宋时的中秋之夜，显贵人家都装扮隆盛，结伴于亭台楼榭，临轩赏月；普通平民则争相占坐酒楼以观月；儿童们连夜嬉耍，夜市热闹异常，通宵达旦，方才罢休。清代时，民间不少地方流行“走月亮”的活动。这天夜晚，妇女们装束隆重，邀请三两个好友一起于中秋之夜出游。直到天快亮、鸡啼鸣之时，依旧在月下行走。

Chang'e Floating to the Moon

People look up to the sky and enjoy the beautiful moon on the night of Mid-Autumn Festival night. There are stories told generations by generations in folklore, and the story of *Chang'e Flying to the Moon* is a particularly interesting one.

It is said that in ancient times, there were ten suns which led to the parched soil, drying up the sea and numerous people dying of thirst and hotness. And a hero named *Houyi* decided to free mankind from the insupportable burden of the existence of the ten suns. He climbed to the top of the *Kunlun* Mountain, and drew his bow with his magic power and shot nine arrows to the suns, leaving only one sun shining over the earth. The people were all thankful to him and a large number of people came to learn skills from him. However, one of them named *Pangmeng* had ulterior motives. *Houyi* always stayed side by side with *Chang'e*, his beautiful wife, except when he went out for hunting and teaching others skills. Watching this affectionate couple, people were all filled with envy. One day *Houyi* obtained an elixir of immortality from the Queen Mother, who told him that he would become an immortal after taking it.He could not tear himself away from his wife,so he gave the elixir to *Chang'e* and

嫦娥奔月

中秋之夜，人们仰望星空，面对那一轮皎月，民间传诵着许多神话故事，尤以“嫦娥奔月”的故事最为人们所津津乐道。

传说远古的时候，天上有一次出现了十个太阳，大地因此而干裂，海水因此而枯竭，百姓们的日子苦不堪言，被渴死、晒死的人不计其数。这时有一个名叫后羿的英雄，立志为百姓除害。他登上昆仑山的顶端，以盖世的神力拉开了神弓，一口气射下了九个太阳，只留一个太阳普照大地。百姓遂对后羿感恩戴德，也有不少人前来向后羿学习技艺。但是其中也混进了一个心术不端的人，名叫逢蒙。后羿有一个美丽善良的妻子名叫嫦娥。平时，后羿除了传授技艺，出外狩猎之外，便是终日伴妻左右。人们对这一对恩爱夫妻非常艳羡。有一天，后

asked her to conceal it. *Pangmeng*, who harbored evil intentions, knew about this. He stayed home under the excuse of illness while *Houyi* and his disciples were all going out for hunting. Then he broke into *Houyi*'s house and forced *Chang'e* to hand over the elixir. Knowing that she might no longer protect the elixir, *Chang'e* took the elixir in a hurry. Suddenly she seemed to get lighter and lighter and flew to the moon. But she missed *Houyi* so much that she had to land at one spot on the moon which was the nearest to the earth. Coming back in the evening and finding out the ins and outs of the matter, *Houyi* went to kill *Pangmeng*, while he had escaped already. What *Houyi* could do was watch the moon and called his wife's name. At that time, it came to him that the moon was especially bright and it seemed that a figure like *Chang'e* was shaking in it. He had an incense table arranged in the back garden that *Chang'e* liked, and prepared her favourite fresh fruit on it, hoping that *Chang'e* who lived lonely in the moon could receive the love and care from him. Knowing that *Chang'e* had flown to the moon, ordinary people all followed after *Houyi* by getting all the offerings prepared and praying for peace and safety from *Chang'e*.

羿在机缘巧合之下向王母娘娘求了一包长生不死之药。据王母娘娘说，服下此药便能即刻成仙。但后羿想到妻子嫦娥，很难割舍。只是暂时收起了不死药，不去想成仙的事，甚至把不死药交给了嫦娥，嘱咐她好生藏好。但此事却被心怀不轨的逢蒙知道了。一次，在后羿带领众多徒弟出外狩猎之时，逢蒙借口身体不适而留了下来。待得后羿等一众人走后，逢蒙便执剑闯入后羿的内宅，逼迫嫦娥交出不死药。嫦娥清楚自己保不住不死药，但又不能让贼人得逞，情急之下，遂一口吞下了不死药。顷刻间，嫦娥的身体变得轻飘飘，渐渐飘离地面，向天空飞去。但多情的嫦娥挂念着后羿，便飞落在离人间最近的月亮之上。傍晚，后羿回到家中，原原本本地知道了来龙去脉，便愤怒地提剑去杀逢蒙，却扑了空，早已让

As *Chang'e* has been given the role of goddess of the moon, she is considered as an immortal who dominates the marriages of the ordinary people. Therefore, the match-makers are also called the old man under the moon in folklore.

Clay Rabbit

There is a rabbit living with *Chang'e*, leading a desolate life in the moon. A story tells that a man named *Wu Gang* had been away from home and studied magic for three years. However, his wife, *Yuanfu*, had fallen in love with *Boling*, grandson of Emperor *Yan*

其遁逃了。伤心的后羿只能仰望月亮，痛呼爱妻的名字。此时的他突然觉得夜晚的月亮特别明亮，且里面似乎有个形似嫦娥的身影在晃动。后羿便差人立刻去嫦娥喜爱的后花园，摆上案几，放上些嫦娥爱吃的蜜食鲜果，希望独自一人在凄冷月宫中寂寞度日的嫦娥，能享受到自己的这一份关怀。老百姓们得知嫦娥奔月成仙后，也效仿后羿，在月下设案，摆放祭品，并向嫦娥祈祷平安。

由于嫦娥被赋予了月神的角色，民间认为嫦娥是主宰人间姻缘的神仙，因此，又将媒人称为"月下老人"。

兔儿爷

月宫中与嫦娥凄清度日的还有一只玉兔。那么，月宫为什么会有一只兔子呢？这还源于一段有趣的故事。传说有个叫吴刚的人，他学习仙术离开

and they had three children in three years. Afterwards, the truth had been known by the Jade Emperor. *Wu Gang* was also involved and banished to the Moon Palace. Feeling ashamed and regretful, *Yuanfu* sent her two little sons who were said to be in the shape of rabbit to accompany *Wu Gang* in the Moon Palace. Therefore, the essential clay rabbit has been used in the sacrificial ceremony of the Mid-Autumn Festival.

Eating Mooncakes

People usually eat one kind of food called mooncake on Mid-Autumn Festival. There are many legends about the mooncake. It is said that in the *Tang* Dynasty, the first emperor, *Liyuan*, spent the holiday with other common people together. He delightfully waved his hands and held the cake offered by the *Tubo* businessmen. Then he pointed at the moon in the sky and said in a loud voice, "The cake looks just like the moon in the sky." After saying this, he shared the cake with all the soldiers and generals. Hence, the tradition of eat-

家乡已有三年了。炎帝的孙子伯陵与吴刚的妻子缘妇私下产生了感情,缘妇怀孕有三年,而且生了三个孩子。后来,这一事情被玉皇大帝所知,吴刚惨遭牵连,被贬到月宫。缘妇十分愧疚,于是让两个小儿子去月宫陪伴吴刚,据说他们后来都化身为兔子。因此在人们过中秋时,兔子是必不可少的,民间常用"兔儿爷"来祭月。

吃月饼

在中秋节的时候,人们常吃一种名叫月饼的食物。民间有许多关于月饼的传说。据说月饼源于唐代,有一次,唐代开国皇帝李渊在中秋节的时候与百姓共度佳节。他兴高采烈地一边挥手,一边拿着吐蕃商人献上的圆饼,指着天上的明月,高声说道:"这饼就像是天上的月亮。"然后将饼与

ing mooncakes has been passed down until the present day. Meanwhile, it is one essential food for family parties on night of the Mid-Autumn Festival.Family members congregate and enjoy the full moon while eating mooncakes. In some areas, people sitting beside the lake enjoy the beautiful night scene or sail on the lake on that night.

众将士分吃，吃月饼的风俗于是一直沿传至今。在中秋节的夜晚，人们举行家庭宴会，月饼也是必不可少的食品。一家人团聚在一起，边吃月饼边赏月。有的地方，还流行在中秋节的这天，全家人在湖边欣赏夜景，或泛舟湖上。

Having been evolved till now, the mooncake is not only rich in taste, but also in shape. There are also differences in workmanship in different regions. Generally, it can be divided into the *Beijing* style, Canton style, *Su* style and *Chaozhou* style. The mooncake of *Beijing* style, which is noted for vegetarian food, is popular in Northern China, especially in *Beijing* and *Tianjin*. Mooncakes of Canton style, consisting of a sugar base are enjoyed mainly in *Guandong* and nearby areas. Mooncakes of *Su* Style with loose crisp taste was popular in *Jiangsu*, *Zhejiang* and *Shanghai*. While mooncakes of *Chaozhou* style, with a flat shape, is favored in areas of *Chaozhou*, *Shantou*.

月饼发展到今天，其口味有很多种，造型也是五花八门。各地月饼的制作工艺也不尽相同。一般而言，月饼主要有京式、广式、苏式、潮式几种。京式月饼主要在北方等地流行，尤其是北京与天津一带，口味主要以素食见长。广式月饼主要在广东等地流行，以糖为主。苏式月饼主要在江苏、浙江、上海一带流行，口味松酥。潮式月饼主要在潮州、汕头等地流行，月饼较为扁平。

Sending Melon

The Mid-Autumn Festival is a day of supplicating for a baby for families. The tradition of married women holding moon sacrifices has a good run in many areas. To supplicate for a baby, there is another way, which is prevalent in *Hunan* Province of China, sending melon on Mid-Autumn Festival. If one didn't give birth to a baby in a wealthy family several years after marriage, the relatives would be invited to send melons on Mid-Autumn Festival. The chosen melon should be the similar size as the white gourd, meanwhile one needed to keep this matter secret from the owner of the garden. The facial features would be drawn on the melon with color pigment, dressed up like a human figure. Then the elder would be asked to carry the melon in his arm and send it to the wealthy family with music and firecrackers being set off. The elder laid the melon on the bed and covered it with quilt, whispering "Reap as one has sown". After that, all the relatives and friends would be entertained with a great feast by the family praying for a baby. The woman would eat the melon as soon as she gets it, with the hope of having a healthy baby in the coming year.

Mooncake Gambling

Mooncake gambling, an important tradi-

送瓜

中秋节是家人求子心切的节日。在不少地方，已婚的妇女都有祭拜月亮，祈祷早日怀孕的习俗。中国的湖南省还盛行一种求子方法，即中秋节送瓜。倘若殷实之家娶媳妇而数年不怀孕，便邀请亲友在中秋节的时候送瓜。瓜要选类似冬瓜般大小的，还不能让瓜园的主人知道。用彩色颜料绘制像人一样的面目在瓜上，还要给瓜穿上衣服，活像个人形。然后请年长者抱着瓜，吹打着乐器，鸣放鞭炮送到求子之家。年长的人将瓜放在床上，用被子盖好，嘴上还念叨"种瓜得瓜，种豆得豆"，然后求子之家大摆盛宴款待亲朋好友。妇女得到这个瓜后需要立刻吃瓜，以祈祷来年生个健康的宝宝。

博饼

这是一种发源于福

tion on Mid-Autumn Festival, originated in *Minnan* area, *Fujian* and prevalent in regions inhabited by Chinese people such as *Taiwan* and Southeast Asia. On every Mid-Autumn night, relatives and friends will be invited to sit around a large porcelain bowl and throw the dice in it in turns. Six dices will be thrown at a time, and the prize that the thrower deserves is decided by the placement of the dices. This activity is called Mooncake Gambling because the original prize gained is the mooncake to be shared together.

Nowadays, not only mooncakes but also other daily necessities or candies are prepared as prizes. Relatives and friends sit round together in the hope of getting a stroke of good luck.

建闽南地区的习俗,在台湾、东南亚等华人聚居的地区十分流行。每逢中秋之夜,人们便邀上亲朋好友,围坐在一个大瓷碗边上,轮流向瓷碗中掷骰子。一次同时掷6颗骰子,根据骰子的排列组合,从而决定掷者应该得到什么奖品。因为最初的奖品是分饼,所以又称为“博饼”。

如今,中秋博饼不仅仅是分食月饼,人们还将许多日用品或糖果充当奖品。亲朋好友围坐在一起博饼,希望能博得一个好彩头。

The *Chongyang* Festival
重阳节

Chongyang Festival is also known as the September 9th, Double Ninth Festival,Chrysanthemum Festival, Daughter's Festival, Old men's Day, etc.. The 9th day of September in the lunar calendar is not only the day when overseas Chinese feel strongly homesick, but also the day when people pray for longevity.

重阳节，又名“九月九”、“重九节”、“菊花节”、“女儿节”、“老人节”等。农历的九月九日，不仅是海外游子思乡倍浓之时，亦是民间祈祷长寿的节日。

Ⅰ. Origin

The origin of the word *Chongyang* has something to do with the records in *The Book of Changes*. Ancient Chinese believed that nine was the largest *Yang* number, and the ninth day of the ninth lunar month was therefore a double *Yang* day (*Chong* means double in Chinese). The long history of the festival dated back as far as the pre-*Qin* period.

Customs of climbing up mountains, drinking wine, and wearing dogwoods on *Chongyang* Festival for ancient people came from a beautiful legend. A young man named *Huan Jing* lived a happy life with his family in

一、来历

“重阳”一词的由来，与《易经》中的记载有关。古人以为九是阳数，九月初九，日月并阳，两阳相重，故曰“重阳”。重阳节的历史悠久，早在先秦时期就已有之。

古人在重阳节的这一天有登高饮酒、佩戴茱萸的习俗。这一习俗的来历源自一段美丽的传奇故事。东汉时，汝南县有

Eastern *Han* Dynasty. Sudddenly such a misfortune took place in the village that a serious plague was raging so that there were some people falling ill. *Huan Jing*' s parents died of the plague that year. When he was a kid, he was told by adults that there was a devil which would appear and bring plague to people every year in *Ruhe* River. *Huan Jing* was determined to pay respect to a master and learn how to get rid of the devil for the villagers. He started packing up to learn skills from master, and heard that there was an immortal called *Fei Zhangfang* living in the mountain. He got up upon hearing the crow of a rooster to practice his swordsmanship with the *Qinglong* sword for vanquishing demons given by *Fei Zhangfang*. A year passed, one day when he was practising, he was told by *Fei Zhangfang* that the devil in *Ruhe* River would come out on the ninth day of the ninth lunar month this year, and he had to go back to kill the evil for the people. In addition, *Fei* gave him a bag of dogwood leaves and a bot-

一个名叫桓景的小伙子，与一家人快快乐乐地生活在一起。可好景不长，村里发生了不幸的事情，汝河两岸爆发了瘟疫，家家户户均有人病倒。就在这一年，桓景的父母也都病死了。桓景小时候听大人们说，汝河里住着一个魔鬼，每年都要出来游走人间。走到哪里，就要将瘟疫带到那里。桓景决心访师求友学好本领，战胜魔鬼，为民除害。听说在山中住着一个名叫费长房的大仙，他就收拾行装，起程进山拜师学艺。费长房给桓景一把降妖的青龙剑。桓景闻鸡起舞，不分昼夜地练剑。一年又过去了，有一天正当桓景练剑时，费长房走到跟前说："今年九月九日，汝河魔鬼又要出来了。你赶紧回乡

tle of chrysanthemum wine and told him to ask villagers climb up high mountains to avoid the disaster. He returned to his hometown and did as *Fei Zhangfang* told him. On the ninth day of the ninth lunar month he took the villagers to a mountain nearby, distributing the dogwood leaves to everyone and told them to take it with themselves so that the devil would be kept away from them and the chrysanthemum wine was given to them for drinking to protect them from being infected with the plague.

Huan Jing made sure the villagers were settled well before he returned home, sitting in the house with his *Qinglong* sword and waiting for the devil. After a while, with a weird wind blowing and the river roaring, the devil went out of the river and walked through the village, finding no one everywhere. At that moment, he looked up and found that villagers were getting together on the high mountain. He ran to the foot of the mountain but dared not go one step due to the smell of the dogwood and chrysanthemum wine. Then he made his way back to the village. Watching a man sitting in the house, the devil roared and pounced at him. *Huan Jing* fought against at the devil with his sword. After a couple of

为民除害,我给你一包茱萸叶子、一瓶菊花酒,让你家乡父老登高避祸。”桓景回到家乡,召集乡亲,将大仙的话传给各位乡亲。九月九日那天,他领着乡亲们登上了附近的一座山。他将茱萸叶子每人分了一片,说这样随身带上,瘟疫不敢近身。又将菊花酒倒了出来,每人喝了一口,说喝了菊花酒,就可以不染瘟疫了。

桓景将乡亲们安顿好后,就带着他的降妖青龙剑回到家中,独坐屋内,等待恶魔来与其交战。没过一会儿,只听汝河怒吼,怪风旋起。恶魔从水里走出来,来到岸边,穿过村庄,走过千家万户,却始终不见一人。忽然,他抬头看见人们都在高高的山上欢聚。他窜到山下,只觉得酒气刺鼻,茱萸冲肺,不敢登山,于是又转身回到村里。只见一个人正在屋中端坐,于是他怒吼一声,向前扑

rounds, judging that he would be outwitted by *Huan Jing*, the devil scrambled to his feet and ran. *Huan Jing* threw out the *Qinglong* sword immediately to the devil. The sword crossed the devil's heart and slashed him down. From then on, villagers around the *Ruhe* River would never be attacked by the devil. The heroic deeds of *Huan Jing* and climbing up mountains to escape from disaster have been handed on from generation to generation. The custom of climbing up mountains has started on to the *Chongyang* Festival from then on.

去。桓景一见恶魔扑来，便急忙舞剑迎战。斗了几个回合，恶魔战胜不过他，遂拔腿就跑。桓景"嗖"的一声将降妖青龙剑抛出，只见宝剑闪着寒光向恶魔追去，穿心透肺将恶魔刺倒在地。此后，汝河两岸的百姓，再也不受恶魔的侵害了。人们将九月九日登高避祸、桓景用剑刺恶魔的英雄事迹，父传子，子传孙，一直传到现在。从那时起，人们过起重阳节来，此后便有了重九登高的习俗。

II. Customs

There are various customs in the *Chongyang* Festival in folklore and the most popular ones are going outing and ascending a height, eating *Chongyang* cakes, wearing a dogwood, appreciating the chrysanthemum, drinking chrysanthemum wine, offering sacrifice to sea-god, married daughters returning home to see parents, and respecting the aged people, etc..

二、习俗

民间在重阳节的这天，有异彩纷呈的庆祝活动。最常见的莫过于登高野游、吃重阳糕、佩戴茱萸、赏菊花、饮菊花酒、祭海神、出嫁女归宁、敬老等活动。

Going outing and Ascending a Height

In ancient times, there was an activity of climbing up mountains on *Chongyang* Festival. Thus the festival is also called *Denggao* Festival since the activities of ascending a height started from *Wei-Jin* North-South period (*Denggao* means ascending a height in Chinese). This activity became more prevalent in the *Tang* Dynasty, when writers and poets climbed up hills, ascended a height and made poetry with friends. There is no unified rules on climbing up. Generally, people climb up mountains or towers. Ascending a height is full of poetic and idyllic romance. The Fragrant Hill in *Beijing*, Cattle Hill in *Shandong*. and the Pavilion of Prince *Teng* in *Nanchang* are all famous interests of places for height ascending. People could feast their eyes on the beautiful scenery in autumn and breathe the fresh air while climbing. Moreover, it is an effective way suitable for people of all ages to keep fit.

Eating *Chongyang* Cakes

The *Chongyang* cake is a kind of food for people to enjoy on *Chongyang* Festival. It is al-

登高野游

古时候，在重阳节的这一天有登高的活动。重阳节登高的活动源于魏晋南北朝时期，重阳节于是又被称为“登高节”。重阳登高之风在唐代更为流行。尤其是许多文人墨客每当重阳节之时，便登高远眺，与朋友一起以诗会友。登高的习俗并无统一的规定，一般是登高山或登高塔。登高被认为是一件富有诗情画意的事情。北京的香山、山东的牛山、南昌的滕王阁都是举世闻名的登高胜地。人们在登高的过程中，可以尽情地欣赏金秋美景，呼吸清爽的新鲜空气，亦有锻炼身体的功效，是一项老少咸宜的活动。

吃重阳糕

重阳糕是人们在重阳节所吃的一种食品。重

so called flower cakes, chrysanthemum cakes, and five-color cakes. The craftsmanship and flavor diverse in different regions. When the Double Ninth Day is approaching, people of all families make steamed cakes with flour. In order to grow the appetite, pomegranate seeds, chestnuts, ginkgo nuts and pinenut kernels are put on the cake, and sometimes the cake is also made in the shape of small animals. These cakes are taken by people as necessary dessert during their climbing.

Wearing Dogwoods

On the Double Ninth Festival, people in every family will wear dogwoods, making it a custom. Therefore, the Double Ninth Festival is also called the Dogwood Festival. Dogwood's smell is useful in deworming, dewetting, wind pathogens dispelling, accumulated fed eliminating and cold curing,etc.. The *Wu* Dogwood, *Yuejiao* (*Wu* and *Yue* are ancient names of some areas in *Jiangnan*) abounding in *Jiangnan* are of high quality. It is considered by people that the Double Ninth Day is a time to turn bad luck into good, and they ought to

阳糕，又名"花糕"、"菊糕"、"五色糕"等，各地的制作工艺与风味各不相同。在重阳节来临之际，家家户户以面粉蒸糕。糕上还点缀有石榴子、栗子黄、银杏、松子仁等果实，或是用糕做成各类小动物的样子置于糕上。重阳节时，人们随身携带这类糕点，作为登高必备的点心。

插茱萸

九月九日重阳节之时，家家户户都要插茱萸，并且成为一种民间习俗。所以重阳节，又名"茱萸节"。茱萸的香气有驱虫去湿、祛除风邪及消积食、治寒热等功效。尤以江南一带盛产的茱萸为上品，故名"吴茱萸"、"越椒"等。民间以为九九重阳这天，乃是逢凶化吉之日，应佩戴茱萸以辟

wear dogwoods to ward off bad luck or disasters. It was very common to see people wear dogwoods on Double Ninth Day in *Tang* Dynasty. Someone wore it on their arms, someone wore it on the sachet around his or her waist, someone even put it directly in the temples. Most of the people wearing dogwoods were women and children. Men could also wear them.

邪去灾。重阳节插茱萸的习俗在唐代十分常见。人们或佩戴于手臂上，或制囊佩戴于腰间，甚至有直接插于鬓角的。妇女、儿童佩戴较多，男子也可佩戴。

Appreciating Chrysanthemum and Enjoying Chrysanthemum Wine

September is the time when chrysanthemums bloom luxuriantly, therefore, it is called the Chrysanthemum Month. The custom of eating chrysanthemum wasrecordedin *Quyuan's* poem *Lisao*, as people believe the chrysanthemum can prolong their life, which has become a mascot in people's pursuing of a long life for its wonderful medicinal properties. Its auspicious meaning helps it guard against the evil, being equally important as the dogwood. Chrysanthemum appreciating had become one of the important customs as early as the *Jin* Dynasty. A saying in *Tang* Dynasty goes that it has to *Chongyang* Festival without

赏菊花与饮菊花酒

每年九月，正值菊花盛开之时。九月在民间又有“菊月”的别称。屈原所著的《离骚》诗中，就记载了民间食用菊花的习俗。因为在古人看来，菊花有延年益寿的功效，因其神奇的药用价值，已成为人们追求长寿的吉祥物。菊花所具有的吉祥寓意，自然成为重阳节的辟邪之物，并与茱萸同等重要。赏菊早在晋朝之时，成为重阳节的重要习俗之一。至唐

the chrysanthemum, thus, the *Chongyang* Festival is also called the Chrysanthemum Day. The chrysanthemum is a very tender, beautiful, graceful and pleasant ornamental flower. Nowadays, all kinds of chrysanthemum shows will be held to increase the festive atmosphere every *Chongyang* Festival.

Offering Sacrifice to Sea-god

There is a prevalent belief in *Mazu* that this god will bring good luck to people in ocean voyages in regions of the southeast coast of China. The Double Ninth Day is the time when the sea-god *Mazu* ascends to heaven, therefore, grand gatherings for offering sacrifice to sea-god will be held every *Chongyang* Festival.

The real *Mazu*, named *Lin Moniang* was born in the the Northern *Song* Dynasty.The kind-hearted girl often removed difficulties, alleviated sufferings for folks. Moreover, she always taught people to do good and led them to pursue good fortune and avoided disaster. Since she lived near the coast, she was good at swimming. She often offered help to sea-going ships, so people called her Godness or Dragon Princess. However, when she was twenty-eight years old, she laid down her young life in saving her brother and father in a

则是无菊不重阳,故重阳节又有“菊花节”的别称。菊花也是一种十分美丽的观赏植物,婀娜多姿、娇艳动人,令人赏心悦目。如今人们每到重阳的时候,还要举办各类菊展,以增添节日的气氛。

祭海神

在中国的东南沿海地区,人们普遍信仰妈祖,认为这一神灵能给在外洋远行的人们带来好运。九月九日是海神妈祖升天的日子,所以每逢重阳节之时,都要举办祭祀海神的盛会。

妈祖的真名叫林默娘,生于北宋年间。林默娘心地善良,经常帮助乡邻,为乡亲们排忧解难,教导人们行善,引导他们避凶趋吉。她因生活在海滨,熟习水性,为航海船只提供帮助,故深受沿海船户的爱戴,人们称她为“神女”、“龙女”。但在她28岁的那一年,因解救出海遭难的父亲与兄

disaster when their outing in the sea. Then she was honored as Sea God after her death. Double Ninth Day is a time when *Mazu* is raised to heaven, so all rituals will be taken place and all kinds of vegetables and fruits will be shown as sacrificial offerings.

Married Daughters' Returning Home

The Double Ninth Day is also the day when married daughters return home to see parents. Therefore, it is also called Daughter's Day. The deed that married daughters return home to see their parents or parents bring daughters back home to eat *Chongyang* cakes has finally developed into a custom.

Respecting the Aged People

The Double Ninth Day is also regarded as seniors' Day. Since the number nine is the biggest number, it is made with the implied meaning that all elders have good health and longevity. Therefore, the Chinese national tradition of showing respect to the old and cherishing for the young has been carried forward.

弟，献出了自己年轻的生命，死后被人们奉为“海神”。九月九日的重阳恰逢妈祖升天之日，这天民众要举行各种仪式，陈列各式蔬菜、瓜果，以便祭拜妈祖。

出嫁女归宁

重阳这天也是出嫁的女儿回娘家的日子，故又有了“女儿节”的别称。出嫁女回家看望双亲，娘家接出嫁的女儿回家吃重阳糕，已发展成节日习俗。

敬老

在中国的法定节日中，重阳节被定为老人节。之所以将重阳节定为老人节，实际上是取“九”这个最大数，寓意老人健康长寿，从而发扬中国人尊老爱幼的民族传统。

The Winter Clothing Day
寒衣节

Winter Clothing Day, as well as Tomb-sweeping and *Zhongyuan* Festival, is one of the festivals for people to offer sacrifices to ancestors. It falls on the first day of lunar October in China. According to the changing regularity in different seasons, October is at the turn of winter. In Northern China, October 1st of the lunar calendar is a symbol of the entering into the cold winter. According to the Chinese tradition, people will send clothes to the relatives to prevent them from being caught a cold. As the time goes, the festival has become a day for people to offer sacrifices to ancestors and send paper clothes to pay homage to the dead.

寒衣节与清明节、中元节，同属民间祭祀祖先的节日。每年的农历十月初一，就是寒衣节。按照四季变化的规律，十月是秋冬交替的时节。在中国的北方，农历的十月初一，已经昭示着将进入寒冷冬季的第一天。依照中国的传统，这天要给亲人送上御寒的衣服。随着时间的推移，寒衣节成为人们祭祀逝者，为逝者送寒衣的节日，以表达对逝者的纪念与崇敬之意。

Ⅰ.Origin

In the ancient times, when it came to the Winter Clothing Day, women would make thick cotton clothes to the relatives to keep out the cold. If the relatives had been dead, people would make clothes with paper, and burn it in

一、来历

在中国古代的时候，每逢寒衣节来临之际，妇女们都要亲自缝制厚厚的棉衣，给远方的亲人御寒。如果亲人已经去世，

front of the grave on this day. And that is why it is called Winter Clothes Day.

则要用纸做成衣服的样式，然后在寒衣节的这天，到亲人的坟前烧掉，所以称之为“寒衣节”。

The Winter Clothing Day is linked with a sad beautiful love story. It is said that in the *Qin* Dynasty, the *Qin Shihuang* united China and built a new country. But he was a man who led a luxurious and dissipated life. He recruited laborers all over the country to construct the Great Wall and his own grave. In the beautiful south of the *Yangtze* River, there lived a family with the family name *Meng*. The old couple loved each other so deeply that there was nothing that could separate them apart. In their leisure time, they made poems or paintings in the back yard. They planted a big gourd in the yard. The leaves were rich and the branches were strong. Because the branches were so long that they stretched over the wall and into the neighbor's yard. By coincidence, the neighbor, *Jiang*, had a big gourd soon after too. In the autumn of a year, *Meng* said to *Jiang*, "Let's cut the gourd into half for each family." When they cut it, they found a white and fat girl inside. Both of the two families loved the girl very much. After discussion, they came to the conclusion that *Meng* brought up the girl and the girl was named *Meng*

寒衣节的由来与一个凄美的爱情故事有关。相传在秦朝的时候，秦始皇统一中国，建立了新的国家。但是秦始皇是一个骄奢淫逸之人，他从全国各地招募劳力去修筑长城与自己的陵墓。在美丽的江南，有一户姓孟的人家。这对老夫妻十分恩爱，亲密无间，闲暇之余，便在自家的后院里作诗或画画。这户人家的院子里，种了一个大葫芦。叶子十分茂盛，枝蔓特别粗壮。由于枝蔓很长，竟然顺着墙爬到了隔壁一户姓姜的人家。巧合的是，没过多久，姓姜的人家院子里结了一个大葫芦。一年秋天，孟家对姜家说：“我们将这个葫芦劈成一半吧，你家一半，我家一半。”当他们切开葫芦时发现，这个葫芦里竟然有一个白白胖胖的女娃

Jiangnü. *Meng Jiangnü* was the most obedient girl, and she took good care of the two families especial. the old so they loved her very much. One day, when she was trying to salvage a fan in the pool, a young man called *Fan Xiliang* passed by and saw this scene. *Fan Xiliang* helped *Meng Jiangnü* to get the fan, and she thanked him very much. She took a close look at the handsome young man, then chatted with him, gradually she fell into love with him. Under *Meng Jiangnü*' s parents' approval, they got married as a couple.

When they were performing the formal wedding, the army broke in and took *Fan Xiliang* away. *Fan Xiliang* was recruited by *Qin Shihuang* as a laborer to build the Great Wall far away. However, after *Fan Xiliang* was caught, *Meng Jiangnü* missed her husband day and night sadly. It snowed heavily outside on October 1st. *Meng Jiangnü* was staring at the

娃。两家人都十分喜欢这个女娃娃。经过商议，由孟家负责抚养女娃娃。双方经过协商，给这个女娃娃取名叫孟姜女。孟姜女是个十分孝顺的女孩子，他对孟家与姜家的老人都十分照顾，特别讨人喜欢。一天，孟姜女在花园的池塘边打捞一把落在水中的扇子。就在这个时候，被一个路过的叫范喜良的青年看见。范喜良帮助孟姜女将扇子打捞起来，孟姜女十分感谢他。孟姜女仔细地看了看这个英俊的青年，然后与范喜良亲切地交谈起来，渐渐的，孟姜女爱上了范喜良。经过孟姜女父母的同意，范喜良与孟姜女结为了夫妻。

正当新婚夫妇拜堂成亲的时候，官兵闯了进来，将范喜良抓走。原来，范喜良被秦始皇征用为民工，要去很远的地方修筑长城。范喜良被抓走后，孟姜女日夜思念自己的丈夫，心情十分悲痛。

candle. Watching the snow, she recalled that when her husband was caught, he hadn't taken any warm clothes with him to keep out cold. Meng Jiangnü wiped her tears away. In order to protect her husband from cold weather, she made a cotton coat in one night and decided to send it to her husband. She packed the coat into the bag and took some money. After bidding farewell to the parents, she left home in sadness. She suffered a lot on her way. Under the help of the good people, finally *Meng Jiangnü* reached the construction site, but the workers told her sadly that *Fan Xiliang* died of overload and his body had been buried under the Great Wall. Hearing this, *Meng Jiangnü* cried out, and slapped the Great Wall. She cried out her husband's name, and accused *Qin Shihuang*'s cruelty. Her cry had moved the heaven and the earth. Suddenly, the strong wind blew up, and lighting accompanied by peals of thunder. With a loud sound, the sky and the earth rifted, one part of the Great Wall cracked, and a pile of white bones showed up. *Meng Jiangnü* cried beside the bones for several days. Then she burnt the coat which then flew up with the wind, surrounded *Meng Jiangnü* for three times, and fell down onto the bones.

十月初一的这一天，外面下起了鹅毛大雪。孟姜女对着蜡烛发呆，眼看外面大雪纷飞，想到自己的丈夫临走的时候，连一件冬天御寒的棉袄都不曾穿在身上，她伤心地擦干了眼泪。为了让自己的丈夫能抵御冬天的严寒，孟姜女连夜做好了一件棉袄，准备将棉袄送给自己的丈夫。孟姜女将棉袄放在袋中，然后带上了一些盘缠，告别父母后，痛苦地离开了家门。一路上，孟姜女受尽了苦难。在许多好心人的帮助下，她终于来到了修造长城的工地旁。但是大家悲痛地告诉孟姜女，她的丈夫早已经活活地累死了，尸骨就埋在了长城之下。孟姜女一听后，不禁号啕大哭，边哭边用双手拍打长城，痛苦地大声喊着范喜良的名字。孟姜女一边为自己惨死的丈夫叫冤，一边无情地控诉着秦始皇的残暴。孟姜女悲痛的哭声，

The story that *Meng Jiangnü* sent the warm coats to her husband thousands of miles away has moved a lot of people. In memory of her, people set October 1st as the Winter Clothing Day. On this day, people cut the colorful paper into clothing, and burn it in front of the relatives' graves to give expression of their grief over the dead's death.

感动了天地。正在这个时候，只看见天空中狂风大作，雷电交加。突然，轰隆一声巨响，顷刻间天崩地裂，一段长城塌掉了。塌掉的长城下，露出了一具白骨。孟姜女守着白骨一连哭了七天七夜，然后将寒衣烧掉了。只见寒衣缓缓地随风飘起，又围绕着孟姜女转了三圈，最后便稳稳地落在了白骨之上。

孟姜女万里寻夫送寒衣的故事，感动了无数的人。为了纪念孟姜女，人们将每年的十月初一定为寒衣节。在这一天，人们要用彩色的纸剪成衣服，然后前往亲人的坟墓前，将纸做出的衣服烧掉，以寄托对死去亲人的哀思。

II. Customs

Burning the Winter Clothing

The day before October 1st, the elders will take the family to add soil to the ancestors' graves. According to the custom, the soil has to be carried with clothes instead of a bas-

二、习俗

烧寒衣

每逢十月初一的前一天，全家人都会在长辈的带领下去祖宗的坟前添土。依照民间的习俗，

ket. Therefore, on this day, everyone carries soil with their clothes. More soil proves more family members. On October 1st, under the leadership of the patriarch, male members of the whole family carry rich sacrificial offerings to the ancestors' graves for the memorial ceremony. The most important thing after the ceremony is to burn the winter clothing. Long before this day, people had cut the colorful paper into clothes full of cotton inside. It is said that the dead can take this as coats or cotton quilts. In the Chinese tradition, only burning these could make the paper things be delivered to the dead. And all must be burned completely. If there is any pieces left, it cannot reach the deceased.

添土不能用箩筐装，必须要用衣服装。于是一家人去添土的时候，每个人都会用衣服兜着土。如果谁家兜的土多，就证明这个家族人丁兴旺。十月初一这一天，在族长的带领下，全家族的男性要抬着丰盛的供品逐个到祖宗的坟前祭拜，以寄托对先祖的哀思。祭拜仪式结束后，最重要的一件事便是烧寒衣。早在寒衣节之前，人们便用彩色纸剪成衣服的样式，并在里面塞入棉花，据说这样可以给亡故者当棉衣或棉被使用。在中国人的传统观念中，只有将冥物焚烧之后，才能真正送到阴间给亡故者使用，而且必须烧得干干净净，倘若有一点没有烧干净，也是无法送到阴间的。

Besides burning the paper clothes, people usually send the cotton coats to the people to see the winter out. In some regions, women give a new cotton coat to their children on Winter Clothing Day in order to help them to prepare for the cold winter. If the weather is

民间除了给亡故者烧寒衣之外，也要给生者送棉衣过冬。在不少地方，妇女们在寒衣节的这天，要给家中的儿女送上棉衣，让他们做好抵御严

warm and not suitable for the cotton coats, women would ask their children to try it on to bring good luck to them. The host will clean the chimney or the fireplace to ensure that the family can keep warm with them when winter comes.

寒的准备。如果这个时候，天气还比较燥热，不适宜穿上棉衣，妇女们也会让儿女们试穿下，以图个吉利。家中的男主人，则要在这一天清理烟囱或是壁炉，以保证冬天来临之时，能够顺利用它们来取暖。

Eating Jumby Bean

In the south of China, people will eat one bowl of jumby bean on this day. It is said that this custom originated from one moving story. Long long ago, there was a cute child cowherd. He had such a poor family that he was not able to be brought up by his parents. So they sent him to the landlord to take care of the cattle. One day, due to his carelessness, the cattle fell into the valley and died. After knowing this, the landlord was so angry that he beat and scolded the boy. Regardless of the boy's begging, the landlord hadn't stopped. Feeling that he was going to be beaten to death, the boy took out a knife and killed the landlord. The boy's blood dyed the rice on the ground into red. And the date

吃红豆饭

在中国的南方，人们在这一天要吃一碗红豆饭。据说这一习俗，源于一个感人的故事。传说在很久以前，有个可爱的放牛娃。这个放牛娃的家中十分贫穷，父母无力抚养他，于是便让他给地主放牛，讨口饭吃。有一天，放牛娃因为疏忽大意，竟然让牛失足掉入山谷之中摔死了。地主知道这件事情后十分生气，于是不停地打骂放牛娃。放牛娃尽管苦苦哀求，地主却并没有停手。放牛娃眼见自己就要被打死了，于是从身边拿出一把刀，将地主砍死。放牛娃的鲜血将撒在

on which it took place was October 1st. In order to remember the boy, people eat the jumby bean on this day.

地上的米饭染成红色。这天正巧是十月初一，人们为了纪念这个放牛娃，于是每到这个时候都要吃一碗红豆饭。

Burning the Paper Money

烧纸钱

The Winter Clothing Day is a day to offer sacrifices to the ancestors. On the morning of the day, the whole family shall go to the ancestors' graves to burn the paper money and pray for ancestors' blessing and protection. According to the folk story, sacrifices and burning the paper money on Winter Clothing Day related to the story of *Cai Lun*'s invention of paper.

寒衣节是祭祀祖先的节日。这天清晨，全家要前往祖先的坟茔烧纸钱，焚香祷告，以祈求祖先的保佑。据民间流传，寒衣节祭祖烧纸钱与蔡伦造纸的故事有关。

According to the historian's research, paper was invented by *Cai Lun*. On the basis of the former experience, *Cai Lun* used tree barks, fish nets, and fibers to make paper. After *Cai Lun* invented the paper, many people came to buy the paper, and the business turned prosperous. In order to expand the business, the family set up a paper factory. But the paper made by *Cai Lun*'s brother, *Cai Mo*, was not good in quality and could not be sold out. *Cai Mo*'s wife, *Huiniang*, cudgeled her brain for ideas of helping her husband out of the difficulty. One night, *Huiniang* pretended to get sick and die. *Cai Mo* was heart-broken. In

据历史学家考证，纸是一个叫蔡伦的人发明的。蔡伦在总结前人经验的基础上，用树皮、渔网、麻等原料制成了纸。蔡伦发明纸以后，很多人都来购买纸张，一时间生意特别好。蔡氏为了扩大经营规模，全家人开设了一家造纸厂。但蔡伦哥哥蔡莫所制造的纸张，质量不好，根本就卖不出去。为此，蔡莫的妻子慧娘冥思苦想，希望能帮助她的丈夫解脱

front of her coffin, *Cai Mo* burnt the paper and said, "I am intending to learn how to make paper with my little brother. But I am not so dedicated. The quality of the paper is so bad that it makes you disappointed and pisses you off. Now I am burning the paper into ash to dissolve your hatred." After one pile of paper was burnt down, *Cai Mo* went to fetch another pile. Just at this moment, *Huiniang* hit the coffin and shouted, "Open the coffin. I am back." This scared the people around. People opened the coffin slowly. And *Huiniang* climbed out of it and said to them, "People' s paper in this world is money for the dead. If the paper is not burnt and changed into money for the dead, no one would send me back. I went to the hell and saw the leader of the ghost. He would have made me suffer in the hell, but my husband turned the paper into the hell money to bribe the ghost so that they opened the back door and released me."

困境。一天夜里，慧娘假装得了疾病，装病死去。蔡莫悲痛欲绝，在她的棺材前痛哭不已，他边烧纸边哭道："我本想跟弟弟好好学习造纸，但是自己却不用心，怎奈造的纸张质量太差，竟然把你气死了。我现在将这些纸烧成了灰，以解你心头之恨。"眼见一堆纸烧完了之后，蔡莫又去抱了一堆纸继续烧。正在这个时候，只听见慧娘不停地拍着棺材，大声喊道："赶紧把棺材打开，我已经回来了。"这可把周围的人吓个半死。人们将棺材缓缓地打开，只见慧娘慢慢地爬起身来，对大家说道："阳间的纸就是阴间的钱，不将纸烧掉，变成阴间的冥币，谁肯把我放回家来？我去了阴间，见了阎罗王一面。阎罗王本要让我去地狱受苦，但是丈夫将阳间的纸变成了阴间的钱，我用这些钱去贿赂了那些小鬼，小鬼就打开了地狱的后门，把我

After hearing this, *Cai Mo* was very surprised and said to his wife, "Will the paper burnt be the money for the dead?" *Huiniang* nodded in agreement. So *Cai Mo* hurried to take several piles of paper and burned for his parents. People around them started to buy *Cai Mo*' s paper. The story spread around very quickly. People far away came to buy the paper and burnt it to their deceased relatives. After a few days, the stock of paper was sold out. Since the day when *Huiniang* came back from the hell was October 1st in the Chinese lunar calendar, people began to offer sacrifices to the ancestors on that day every year, and burn paper in order to worship the dead relatives.

放了回来。"

蔡莫听后，十分惊讶，他对妻子说道："难道阳间的纸，烧了以后就会变成阴间的钱。"慧娘欣然点头。就这样，蔡莫赶紧抱着几捆纸，烧给他已经亡故的父母亲。在场的人一听后，便都纷纷购买蔡莫的纸。这一故事很快就在周边传开来了。不少人从很远的地方赶到蔡莫家，购买他家制作的纸，烧给亡故的亲人。没过几日，积压一时的纸，很快就被抢购一空。因为慧娘从阴间回到阳间的那一天，正好是农历的十月初一。所以，后人每逢十月初一的那天，都要祭祀自己的祖先，并通过烧纸的方式，缅怀死去的亲人。

The Winter Solstice Festival
冬至节

Winter Solstice, which falls on between December 21 and 23, is an important day marking one of the twenty-four divisions of the solar year in the traditional Chinese lunar calendar. It is also a traditional folk festival with the name Winter Festival which predicts the coming of winter. As a saying goes, Winter Solstice Festival is as important as the Spring Festival. In ancient times, people spent the Winter Solstice Festival as ceremoniously as they did in the Spring Festival.

冬至是中国农历重要的节气之一,也是传统的民间节日。俗称“冬节”等,本意就是冬天来了。冬至一般在每年公历的12月21日至23日之间。在古代,人们过冬至与过春节一样隆重,民间俗称“冬至大如年”。

Ⅰ.Origin

Winter Solstice was just a solar term at the beginning. According to the record of ancient literature, the shining time of sun is the shortest and the shadow on the ground is the longest on that day. Thereby it is called Winter Solstice. But there is another saying that the origin of the Winter Solstice relates to *Yin* and *Yang*, a notion of Chinese philosophy (*Yin* means cold, poor,etc.; *Yang* means warm,

一、来历

冬至最初只是一个节气。据古代文献记载,冬至这一天,太阳光照射的时间最短,投射在地面上的影子最长,故名“冬至”。还有人认为,冬至的起源与中国人的阴阳观念有关。在中国人的观念中,阴与阳是生命平衡的

strong, etc.). In Chinese notion, *Yin* and *Yang* are the symbols of the balance of life. Winter Solstice is the coldest and most decisive day of a year. Later, the coldness will be replaced by the brightness of *Yang* gradually, signaling the arrival of spring.

There are many legends about the Winter Solstice Festival. In the north, it is said that one needs to eat *Huntun* (the wonton) in the Winter Solstices and noodles in the Summer Solstice. Legend has it that in the *Han* Dynasty, northern Huns nomadic people often assaulted people living in Central Plains (comprising the middle and lower reaches of the Yellow River). At that time, there were two eminent leaders whose names were respectively *Hun* and *Tun* in Huns tribe. People living in distress hated these two murderous leaders so deeply that they folded meat stuffing and gave it the name *Huntun* (the wonton) blended by the two leaders' name. After that, they ate the wonton to express their abhorrence of war and prayed for a peaceful living. From then on, this custom has been gradually handed down.

Winter Solstice is a grand festival of sacrifice. According to the calendar of the *Zhou* Dynasty, Winter Solstice is the beginning of a new year and the day before Winter Solstice is the end of the last year. In *Zhou* Dynasty, peo-

象征。冬至这一天是阴寒最强之日，是一年最关键的时间。这天过后，阳的光明逐渐取代阴寒，预示着春天的来临。

历史上有许多关于冬至节的传说。在北方，民间有“冬至馄饨、夏至面”的说法。相传在汉朝的时候，北方的匈奴游牧民族经常袭扰中原，百姓不得安宁。当时匈奴部落中有两个声名显赫的领袖，一个名“浑”、另一个名“屯”。中原百姓十分痛恨这两个凶残的首领，于是用肉馅折成角，取“浑”、“屯”之音，名曰“馄饨”。然后将馄饨食入腹中，以表达对战争的痛恨，祈祷能过上太平日子。此后，这一习俗逐渐被流传下来。

冬至节是一个隆重的祭祀节日。依照周代的历法，冬至是新一年的岁首，冬至前一日则是上一年的岁末。在周朝，人们

ple have already had the tradition of celebrating Winter Solstice. On that day, the emperor led ministers to hold a spectacular ceremony of offering sacrifices to gods and ancestors and welcoming the arrival of the New Year in the ancestral temple. Besides, the emperor would hold singing and dancing shows to worship gods and prayed for a favorable climate and a prosperous state in the suburb outside the city. It was not until *Han* Dynasty that the new calendar had been adopted, therefore, Winter Solstice and New Year's Day were separated. However, Winter Solstice was still considered the most important festival. The Emperor of *Han* Dynasty would hold a grand ceremony which was called winter celebration with hundreds of ministers. In folklore, the Winter Solstice is regarded as the beginning of the New Year. Even if poor people would put on new clothes and invite relatives and friends to hold the ceremony of worshipping ancestors and respecting elders at home on that day.

就有过冬至节的习俗。这一天，皇帝要亲自率领大臣前往宗庙，举行盛大的祭祀和迎新仪式。此外，皇帝还要在城外的荒郊边举行歌舞表演，以拜祭天地，祈求来年风调雨顺、国泰安康。汉代的时候，人们采用了新的历法，才将冬至和元旦分开，但仍旧视冬至节为最重要的节日。汉代的皇帝与百官在冬至这一天，要举行隆重的朝贺仪式，称之为“贺冬”。在民间，冬至作为“岁首”的习俗一直被流传下来。即便是贫寒的百姓，在冬至这一天也要穿上新衣服，然后邀集亲朋好友，在家中举行祭祀祖先、拜见长辈的仪式。

Ⅱ. Customs

On Winter Solstice, there are more customs relevant to the farming and diet. In the north, people will kill sheep, eat dumplings and wonton, while those in the south usually eat rice balls and long noodles. In addition,

二、习俗

在冬至节的这天，民间有许多农事和饮食习俗。在北方，人们要宰羊、吃饺子、吃馄饨。在南方，人们则吃米团、吃长线面

dog meat is prepared for food as the custom in many places.

Eating Dog Meat

It is said that the custom of eating dog meat has been handed down from the *Han* Dynasty. *Liu Bang*, an eminent Emperor of *Han* Dynasty, had always been fighting outside year by year. Therefore, he had a nasty taste. A minister named *Fan Kuai* cooked a pot of dog meat soup. Having enjoyed the delicious soup, *Liu Bang* gave unceasing praise for its tasty flavor. After that, this custom has been circulated among the people, who will stew dog meat with different kinds of herbal medicine to nourish body and hope for a good luck in the coming year.

Eating Polished Glutinous Rice with Red Beans

In the south of *Yangtze* River, the whole family get together to enjoy the sweet polished glutinous rice with red beans every Winter Solstice. There is a funny story about this custom that there was a cruel ghost who always did harm to people in the areas around the

等，不少地方还有吃狗肉的习俗。

吃狗肉

据传，吃狗肉的习俗是汉代流传下来的。赫赫有名的汉高祖刘邦，长年在外征战，食之无味。有一个名叫樊哙的大臣，煮了一锅香喷喷的狗肉汤。刘邦吃后，感觉味道特别鲜美，对此赞不绝口。这一习俗后来被流传至民间，人们在冬至这一天，用各种中草药熬制狗肉以滋补身体，以祈求来年有个好兆头。

吃红豆糯米饭

在江南一带，每逢冬至节的夜晚，全家人都要围聚在一起，共同享用甜美的红豆糯米饭。有关这一习俗，还有一个有趣的故事。传说，在江南一带有个凶神恶煞的厉鬼，经常出来残害百姓。街坊邻里一到夜晚，便家家闭户，

south of *Yangtze* River. All neighbors had to close the door and be frightened to go out when night came. But the ghost had a fatal weakness that he was afraid of red beans. Therefore, people eat polished glutinous rice with red beans to drive out the ghost, prevent disasters and get rid of illnesses.

不敢外出。但是这个厉鬼有个致命的弱点，便是害怕红豆。于是，人们在冬至节这一天吃红豆糯米饭，以驱逐厉鬼，防灾祛病。

Eating Dumplings

In *Henan*, people eat Frozen Ears, the dumpling we are familiar with. There is a moving story about the custom. It is said that *Zhang Zhongjing*, known as the medical sage, worked as an official away from home. On Winter Solstice, he retired from office and returned home in *Nanyang*. Watching local people with frozen ears in rags, Zhang *Zhongjing* felt so sad. He took his disciples with him and put up a medical shed outside the downtown. They stewed mutton, cayenne pepper and some medicine which could fend off a chill together. After that the stewed material was chopped finely and put into the flour cover which was shaped like an ear. Finally put them into the pot again and boiled to be the medicine, which can fend off a chill, and distributed to ordinary people for free. After

吃饺子

在河南，人们在冬至节吃“捏冻耳朵”，即我们所熟知的饺子。关于这一食俗，还有一段感人肺腑的故事。相传医圣张仲景在外地为官，冬至这天告老还乡，遂返回南阳老家。眼见家乡的百姓衣不遮体，不少人的耳朵都被冻烂了，张仲景的心里十分难过。张仲景和他的弟子在城外搭起医棚，然后将羊肉、辣椒和一些驱寒的药材放在锅内熬煮，再捞出来剁碎，用面皮包成像耳朵的样子。然后将其再放入锅里煮熟，做成驱寒的药物施舍给百姓。乡亲们服用后，冻耳都被医治好了。后来，当地的百姓就承袭这一习俗，认为

taking the medicine, people' s frozen ears were cured. From then on, local people decided to hand down this custom since they believed it was able to fend off a chill and got rid of illness to eat dumplings.

Eating Rice Cake

The rice cake is a particular Chinese taste snack suitable for both the young and the old. In the South, when it comes to Winter Solstice, people usually eat their favorite rice cakes of different tastes. In the morning, rice cakes with sesame and white sugar are chosen as breakfast. People will eat fried rice cakes full of vegetables, winter bamboo shoots, shredded meat,etc. at lunch time. In the evening, people prefer rice cake soup with vegetables, bamboo shoots and shredded meet. According to the folklore, eating rice cakes can help people grow taller year by year, and desire for good luck.

Eating *Tangyuan*(Glutinous Rice Balls)

Tangyuan, which is popular in many places on the Winter Solstice, is a snack with folk flavor. In many places, people make *Tangyuan* into different shapes such as cat, dog or rabbit to cater for the children. However, *Tangyuan* is originally round.

冬至节吃饺子，可以驱寒祛病。

吃年糕

年糕是中国特有的风味小吃，老少咸宜。在南方，每逢冬至节的时候，人们都特别喜爱吃年糕。人们在这一天，要制作各种不同风味的年糕。在早上，人们吃的是芝麻拌白糖的年糕。中午，人们吃的是油炒年糕，作料有蔬菜、冬笋、肉丝等。夜晚，人们喜欢吃笋丝汤年糕。按照民间的说法，冬至节这天吃年糕，喻示年年长高，以祈求吉祥。

吃汤圆

汤圆是民间传统的风味小吃，不少地方流行冬至节吃汤圆。汤圆本是圆形的，但是在

Moreover, there are something special about eating *Tangyuan*. For instance, one should have *Tangyuan* in pairs each time to expect good luck. If there are only two drops of *Tangyuan* left in the bowl, everything will turn out perfect as married people wish. If there is only one single *Tangyuan* left in the bowl, everything will be smooth for the single people.

不少地方，为了迎合孩子们的要求，人们将汤圆捏成小猫、小狗、小兔子等形状。孩子们每到此时都吃得很高兴。此外，吃汤圆还有不少讲究。譬如，吃冬至汤圆时，必须成双成对地入口，以求吉利。如果吃到最后只剩下两粒汤圆，已婚之人将会万事如意。如果吃到剩下一粒汤圆时，单身未婚者将会诸事顺利。

Presenting Shoes

Presenting shoes is another custom in folklore on the Winter Solstice. It is said that, people had the custom of giving shoes of mandarin ducks as a gift to each other in the *Han* Dynasty. Afterwards, the custom has developed into a tradition that uncle or aunt presents shoes or hats to nephews to express their best wishes. Former embroideries presented to men are made in the shape of a dog or a tiger mostly, with beasts embroidered on it. The gifts for

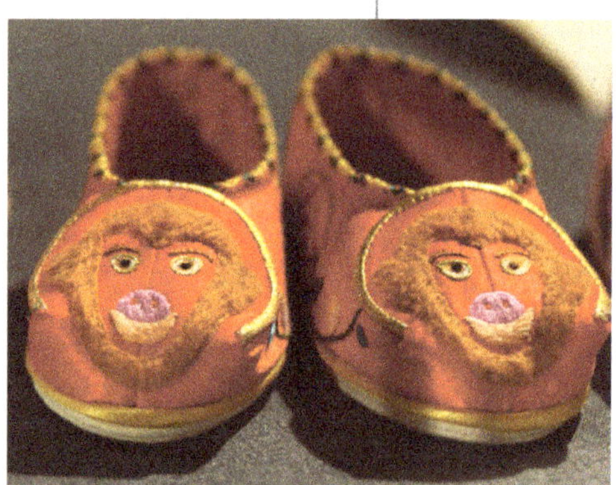

赠鞋

在民间，冬至节有互赠鞋子的习俗。相传在汉代的时候，人们就有互赠鸳鸯鞋的习俗。后来这一习俗逐渐演变为舅姑将鞋帽赠予外甥或侄子，以表达良好的祝愿。在以往的刺绣制品中，给男子送的礼物，多做成虎形或狗形，鞋上多绣的是野兽。送给女

women are made in the shape of a phoenix, with flowers and birds embroidered on it.

子的礼物，多做成凤形，鞋帽上多绣的是花鸟。

Respecting Teachers

尊师

In ancient times, people had the custom of inviting teachers to dinners on Winter Solstice. Students will kowtow to the teacher after the teacher leads the students to worship the memorial tablet of Confucius first. In the folklore of *Shanxi*, there is a prevalent idiom of do the teaching in the Winter Solstice. In many places, it is also very popular to invite teachers to dinner. Especially in the North, stewed mutton is used to entertain teachers.

在古代，冬至节有宴请教书先生的习俗。先生要带领学生祭拜孔子牌位，然后学生再祭拜先生。在山西的民间，还流传着“冬至节教书”的习语。不少地方还盛传冬至节请教师吃饭的习俗。尤其在北方地区，人们习惯用炖羊肉来招待老师。

Drinking Winter Wine

喝冬酿酒

Winter wine is a must on the Winter Solstice for people in *Suzhou*. Winter wine is brewed with rice coupled with sweet osmanthus, the aroma of which is attractive. While drinking winter wine, people will also have pot-stewed food such as spiced beef, spiced mutton and other kinds of pot-stewed food at the same time in the evening. In cold winter, the wine can not only fend off a chill but also embody their good wishes for life in *Suzhou*.

冬酿酒是苏州人在冬至节必饮的一种酒。冬酿酒是一种米酒，加入桂花酿造，香气宜人。姑苏百姓在冬至夜畅饮冬酿酒的同时，还会配以卤牛肉、卤羊肉等各式各样的卤菜。在寒冷的冬天，冬酿酒不仅能够驱寒，更寄托了苏州人对生活的一种美好祈愿。

The *Laba* Festival
腊八节

The *Laba* Festival is a Chinese traditional festival which generally falls on the eighth day of the twelfth lunar month every year. In the folk, the twelfth month is called the *La* month, therefore, the day is called *Laba* Festival (*Ba* has the pronunciation meaning eight in Chinese). The *Laba* Festival is a time of worshiping the ancestors and gods in the hope of a harvest and auspicious luck in the next year. Furthermore, in many places, ceremonies, which is derived from the ancient Chinese *Nuo* culture, are held in the hope of getting rid of disease on that day. In addition, it is also the time for Buddha to be enlightened to Buddhism, therefore, *Laba* Festival becomes a grand festival for Buddhists.

腊八节是中国的传统节日，大体为每年的十二月初八。在民间，人们将农历十二月称之为“腊月”，故俗称“腊八节”。腊八节是人们祭祀祖先和神灵的节日，以祈求来年丰收、吉祥。此外，不少地方在腊八节的那天还要举行驱除疫病的仪式。这项活动源于中国古代的傩文化。在佛教中，佛祖成道的日子也是十二月初八，因而腊八节也是佛教徒的盛大节日。

Ⅰ.Origin

The twelfth lunar month is a period of time for sacrifice at the end of the year. In ancient Chinese society, the worshipping events of the twelfth lunar month had something to do

一、来历

腊月是先民举行年终祭祀的日子。在中国古代社会中，腊月的祭祀活动与农业生产有关。每当

with agriculture. When getting a heavy harvest, people believed it was the outcome of god blessing, so they would hold rites to offer sacrifices to show gratitude to the god. Not only common people, but also the royal family would hold rites to worship gods and pray for a favorable climate and a prosperous state in the next year at the suburb outside the city of *Beijing*.

The activities held during the *Laba* Festival mainly include consecrating gods of heaven, worshipping deities, ancestors and ghosts to avert a disaster. Later the customs of using red beans to hit ghosts and having *Laba* porridge made of nuts and dried fruit were added. The provision on *Laba* Festival may relate to the propagation and faith of Buddhism at that time. It is said the eighth day of the twelfth lunar month is the day when Sakyamuni, the founder of Buddhism, was enlightened, and that day is therefore also called the Festival of Buddha' s Enlightenment. Before his enlightenment, Sakyamuni spent his life on self-denial and mortification for six years when he just had little to eat every day. Later a shepherdess fed him rice and then Sakyamuni got the enlightenment under the bodhi tree. From then on, all temples would make porridge presenting to worshippers all around when it is on

人们获得大丰收之时，便认为这是上天诸神眷顾与庇佑的结果，于是便要举行盛大的祭典仪式。不仅民间百姓有祭祀活动，就连皇家每年也要在京城的郊外举行盛大的祭祀仪式，以祈求来年风调雨顺、国泰民安。

腊八节祭祀主要是供奉天帝、祭祀神灵、祭祀祖先、祭鬼禳灾等，后来又增加了“赤豆打鬼”和吃“腊八粥”等食俗。腊八节的规定可能与当时佛教的传播和信仰有关。相传农历十二月初八是佛祖释迦牟尼成道的日子，称“佛成道节”。佛在成道前曾苦行六年，每日仅食一麻一米，后来一牧羊女供给饭食，佛在菩提树下成道。后来各大佛寺在腊八时做粥馈赠四方善男信女。传到民间，平民百姓也加以效法，用各色杂粮做腊八粥，并逐渐成为习俗。另外，中国民间“赤豆打鬼”的传说

Laba Festival. In the folk, common people imitated and improved the craftsmanship, by using various coarse cereals to make *Laba* porridge, which is gradually developed into a custom. Furthermore, a legend of *Red Bean Hitting the Ghost* in the folk tells that *Gonggong's* son died and became a ghost who could spread plagues. The ghost feared nothing but red beans, so the saying of the red bean of *Laba* hitting ghost came out. The fact that *Laba* porridge is mainly boiled with beans relates to it. Nowadays *Laba* porridge which is stewed with coarse rice, polished glutinous rice, millet and varieties of beans, almond, melon seeds, peanuts and pine nuts is still enjoyed very much by people on *Laba* Festival. Later such famous flavor snack as eight treasures congee (rice pudding) has come out.

讲的是共工的儿子死后变成了撒播瘟疫的鬼，这个鬼天不怕地不怕，单怕赤豆，故有“腊八赤豆打鬼”之说。腊八粥多以豆煮就与此有关。今天的腊八节，人们仍喜欢吃腊八粥，多用黄米、江米、小米以及各种豆类、杏仁、瓜子、花生、松子等熬成，乃至出现了八宝粥这样的风味名吃。

Ⅱ. Customs

On *Laba* Festival, people will not only have *Laba* porridge and hold worshiping rites, but also go out for hunting in order to make up for the insufficiency of food in ancient times. In some places, there is a custom that the hunted beasts should be used as sacrificial offerings to the ancestors in order to pray for happiness, prosperity, longevity and safety of the family.

二、习俗

腊八节的这一天，人们不仅要喝腊八粥，举行祭祀仪式，而且在古代的时候，人们要外出打猎，多储存些食物，以弥补粮食的不足。有不少地方，还将打猎所获取的野兽，作为祭祀祖先的供品，以祈祷来年全家福禄寿齐

Laba Porridge

Laba porridge is the particular food with festival character on *Laba* Festival. There is a moving story about the origin of *Laba* porridge. Once upon a time, a peasant household lived in a remote village, and they had only a son.

This kind-hearted old couple were always ready to bring their own food to help others out of the difficulties when someone met difficulties or someone's granary was nearly empty but the new crop was not yet ripe. As time passes by, their only son had grown up. However, the healthy and strong young man was very lazy. For being spoiled, he consequently didn't like farming at all after growing up. Later he became a dawdler who did nothing but eat and sleep every day. Soon after, the old couple helped their son marry a wife. Unfortunately the girl was the same as the son who was too lazy to do housework and just liked sleeping all day.

全，平平安安。

腊八粥

腊八粥是腊八节特有的节庆食物。有关腊八粥的来历，还有一段感人的故事。相传在很早以前，有一家农户生活在偏远的乡村，他们俩膝下只有一个儿子。

这对老夫妇是心地善良、乐于帮助邻里乡亲的好人。要是谁家有困难，或是庄稼青黄不接之时，他们都愿意将自家的粮食拿出来接济别人，共渡难关。日复一日，年复一年，眼看他们的儿子也长大成人了。可是，这个小伙子虽然长得身强力壮，却是一个好吃懒做之人。由于从小就娇生惯养，因此长大后，就十分讨厌干农活。每天都是游手好闲，除了吃饭就是睡觉，什么活也不干。不久以后，老两口给儿子娶了媳妇。谁知道，媳妇跟儿子一样，同样是好吃懒做，每天就知道睡觉，一

Several years later, the old couple was seriously ill and bedridden. Before passing away, they exhorted the son and daughter-in-law, "If you want to live a good life, don't forget to work diligently. Man does farmwork and woman engages in spinning and weaving." When they had hardly finished speaking, they passed away. The son and daughter-in-law entrusted their neighbors to help them bury their old parents. However, they chose to go back home for sleeping. The son asked his wife, "Look, the rice jar is full of rice and the cabinet is filled with cotton padded clothes. We have enough food and clothes, so why should we farm laboriously in the land?" The daughter-in-law agreed with her husband and said, "The clothes wore in spring and winter are available, so do we really need to spin and weave?" Soon afterwards the young couple forgot the old parents' testament completely. One year later, the land was full of wild grasses. The living necessities were becoming less and less, but the young couple still didn't worry and only they couldn't be bothered to do anything as long as they have a mouthful cooked-rice to eat. Another year has gone by, it came to autumn and every family was busy with a harvest. All foods and clothes have

点家务活也不会干。

过了几年，老爷爷和老奶奶都身患重病，长期卧床不起，于是他们在临死前把儿子和媳妇叫到床前，说道："如果想以后过上好日子，就要勤勤恳恳地做事，男的耕作，女的织布。"话还没有说完，老爷爷和老奶奶就过世了。夫妻俩委托乡亲埋葬了两位老人，自己则返回家中呼呼大睡。儿子对媳妇说道："这米缸里不是还有米吗？这柜子里不是还有棉衣吗？有吃有喝，何必辛苦去田里耕作呢？"媳妇也说："夏天的衣服和冬天的衣服都有了，何必还要纺纱织布呢？"小两口早就把两位老人的遗嘱忘到脑后去了。又过了一年，田地都变成了荒草。家里的生活日用品，也一天天地减少，但是小两口却根本不着急。只要有口饭吃，就懒得动手。又一年过去了，等到秋天的时候，家

been used up, and the lazy couple began to bear starving.For the dead old couple' s sake, the neighbors helped them and gave them steamed bread and soup. Nevertheless, the young couple still believed that they could live even if by begging.

It was becoming colder and colder in the twelfth lunar month. On the eighth day, the temperature was so low that the water had been frozen. The young couple wanted to get warm by making fire in the house, and they hug together tightly and huddled on the *Kang* (one kind of bed in northern part) because they had no clothes or food to keep warm. They searched the whole room with eyes. Suddenly they found several beans in the chink of wall and then dig the beans out one by one with fingers. Later they found extra rice on the ground and picked them up one by one again. For them,the little grain was essential food which can save their lives. They collected the beans and rice which they could find and cooked them in pot, then they put the

家户户都在忙着收庄稼，可他们家里的吃穿已经耗尽了。小两口终日忍饥挨饿，邻居们看在去世老人的面子上，要么这家给个馒头，要么那家给碗汤喝。即便如此，小两口也总是再想，就是讨饭，这日子也勉强过得下去。

进入十二月，天越来越冷了。在初八的这天，天气十分寒冷，水都结成了冰。小两口在屋内没有柴火取暖，身上没有单衣裹身，肚子里也没有粮食，两个人紧紧地抱在一起，蜷缩在炕头上。他们两双眼睛满屋子地搜寻，突然发现在墙的缝隙里有几粒豆子，就用手一粒粒地抠出来。突然发现在地上有几颗米粒，就一点点地挖出来。这些对他们而言，都是救命的粮食。他们东拼西凑，将粮食放在锅里

grass on the *Kang* into the kitchen stove in order to make fire to stew a pot of porridge with mixed grain. The porridge included millet, corn, soybean, sorghum and leaves of vegetable ,etc., whatever can allay hunger. They pitifully had the porridge in haste after boiling. At that moment, the gale unexpectedly came and the house was soon collapsed because of disrepair for many years. Then the young couple was kept under the house. The moment the neighbors came there, they had been dead and left half a bowl of porridge. From then on, when it came to the eighth day of the twelfth lunar month, people of neighborhood would cook a pot of porridge to children and told them the story of grain porridge in order to teach them to become diligent and hardworking. Being handed down till now, it has become a custom of having grain porridge in the eighth day of twelfth lunar month, and it is called *Laba* porridge.

There are varieties of methods to make *Laba* Porridge, which mainly mixes different kinds of ingredients together with the rice to stew into porridge. The ingredients include red

煮。他们将铺在炕上的草放进灶里，就这样熬制出了一锅五谷杂粮都有的粥。这粥里面有小米、玉米、黄豆、高粱、菜叶等，凡是能充饥的都放进去了。煮熟后，一人一碗，可怜兮兮地喝了下去。这时候，一阵大风突然刮来，由于房子年久失修，早已破败不堪，被风一吹，很快就坍塌了。小两口就这样被压在了房屋底下。等邻居们赶来的时候，他们都已经死了，身边还放着半碗杂豆粥。从此以后，乡亲们每到腊月初八的这天，就家家熬制一锅杂粮粥给孩子们吃，并给孩子们讲述杂粮粥的故事，以此来教育他们。流传到今天，也就形成了腊月初八吃杂粮粥的习俗。因为是腊月初八的这天喝粥，所以又称之为“腊八粥”。

腊八粥的做法各种各样，品种繁多，大多是将各种食材，掺在白米中熬制成粥。这些食材主要

dates, lotus seeds, walnuts, almonds peanuts, longans, grapes, rose, red bean and so on. People usually start to prepare on the seventh day of the twelfth lunar month, stewing the porridge with slow fire from midnight until next morning, then the delicious *Laba* porridge is completed. Some *Laba* porridge will be worshipped to the dead ancestors first and others will be presented to the relatives and friends before mid-day. Finally the whole family will have the rest of the porridge. It is a good omen to have remains which means you can get more than you wish for every year. Moreover, it is a kind behavior to show mercy by presenting *Laba* porridge to poor people.

有：红枣、莲子、核桃、杏仁、花生、桂圆、葡萄、玫瑰、红豆等。人们往往在腊月初七的那一天就开始忙碌，半夜的时候用微火慢慢地熬，一直炖到第二天清晨，腊八粥才算熬制好。腊八粥熬好之后，一部分要先敬神祭祖，一部分可用于馈赠亲友，但是一定要在中午之前送出去。最后剩下的才给全家人食用。如果腊八粥吃的还有剩余，留存下来的便是好兆头，取“年年有余”的意思。如果将腊八粥送给穷苦人吃，那便是行善之举。

Laba Tofu

Laba tofu is a particular kind of food in the folk. When it comes to the eighth day of the twelfth lunar month, all families in the country will let tofu be exposed to the sun, and the naturally exposed tofu is called *Laba* Tofu.

腊八豆腐

腊八豆腐是一种民间风味特产。每到腊月初八的时候，在乡村里的家家户户都要晒制豆腐，民间将这种自然晒制的豆腐称作“腊八豆腐”。

Boiling Beans

In some places, people make porridge,

煮豆子

有些地方腊八煮粥，

but they give the name boiling Five Beans instead of *Laba* porridge. Some people make it on the eighth day of the twelfth lunar month, but some make it on the fifth day. While boiling the porridge, people will put beans in it and will send it to neighbors. People in some places will always eat boiled beans until the twenty-third day of the twelfth lunar month, which means having a big harvest year by year.

却不叫煮"腊八粥",而叫做煮"五豆",有的在腊八当天煮,有的在腊月初五就煮好了。不少地方在煮腊八粥的时候,要加入常见的豆类。煮的豆子,除了自己食用外,大部分还要馈赠给乡邻。有的地方,常年吃煮豆子,一直吃到腊月二十三,象征年年有余。

Laba Noodles

On *Laba* Festival, people in the northern part of China will have one kind of food named *Laba* noodles instead of porridge. Usually people will get all kinds of vegetables and fruits prepared to make them into the ingredients, and then cook the noodles with the ingredients the day before *Laba* Festival. Till the morning of the eighth day of the twelfth lunar month, the whole family will have the noodles together.

腊八面

在中国北方地区,在腊八节的时候,人们不吃腊八粥,而是吃一种叫腊八面的食物。一般在腊八节的前一天,人们就用各种蔬菜、水果等制成作料,将面条制作好,然后将作料放入面条之中。到腊月初八早晨的时候,全家围坐在一起吃腊八面。

Chinese New Year's Eve
除夕

Chinese New Year's Eve, the last evening of the lunar year, is the most important traditional festival in China, like the Christmas Eve in western countries. It is also called the thirtieth day of the lunar year which is the most significant day as well as the first day of the lunar year. It is the time for a family reunion. In some places, people usually get together all night and welcome the coming of the New Year, which is called staying-up.

除夕是中国最重要的传统节日。一般指的是农历一年中的最后一天夜晚，其地位与西方的平安夜相似。除夕，又被叫做"大年三十"。大年三十与大年初一是中国人最重要的日子。除夕这一天是一家人团聚的时刻，有的地方人们要通宵聚集在一起，迎接新年的到来，被称为"守岁"。

Ⅰ. Origin

New Year's Eve originated from the ancient Chinese culture called *Nuo* and the worshipping rites of dispelling epidemic. In *Zhou* Dynasty, when it came to the end of a year, people would hold the *Nuo* rite. They wore different kinds of masks of ghosts, monsters or beasts and then dressed up like ghosts to get rid of pestilence. The appellation of Chinese

一、来历

除夕源于中国古代的傩文化，以及祛除疫病的祭祀仪式。在周朝，每逢年终的时候都要举行傩仪式。人们戴上各种鬼怪或野兽的假面具，装扮成鬼兽的样子驱赶瘟疫。到了汉代的时候，除夕这

New Year's Eve was widely spread among the folk when it came to *Han* Dynasty. The custom of staying-up appeared in *Tang* Dynasty. Every New Year's Eve, the whole family got together to chat with each other while having a drink, longing for the arrival of New Year. In *Ming* and *Qing* dynasties, abundant activities in celebrating the Chinese New Year's Eve came out. On that day, some people chose to have dumplings and others had rice cakes and set off firework to celebrate this festival. Since modern times, the Gregorian calendar was used in recording the year. The former government stipulated in law that the first day of the first lunar month is Spring Festival and the day before is Chinese New Year's Eve, and then the days from the first day to the fifteenth day of the first lunar month are called Spring Festival period or celebrating New Year in folklore.

In the folk, there is an interesting story about celebrating New Year. Legend has it that long ago, a fierce and cruel monster called *Nian* with long feelers on its head living under the sea all the year round. Only on every Chinese New Year's Eve, it crawled on the shore to steal the grain in the fields and the livestock in farmers' houses. Sometimes it would even attack human and hurt them to death. There-

一称谓开始在民间广泛流传。唐代的时候，民间已经出现了守岁的风俗。每逢除夕之夜，全家人都要围聚在一起，一边喝酒聊天，一边等待新年的到来。明清的时候，除夕的庆祝活动已经十分丰富了。人们在这天夜晚，要围在一起吃饺子，庆祝新年。有的还要放烟花，吃年糕。近代以来，中国改用公历纪年。当时的政府，从法律上规定每年的正月初一为春节，前一天则叫除夕，并且将正月初一至正月十五日的这些天，统称为春节，民间俗称“过年”。

在民间还流传着一个有关“过年”的有趣故事。传说在很久以前，当时有一种叫“年”的怪兽。这个怪兽长得十分凶狠，头上的触角很长，常年居住在海底。只有每年除夕的时候，才会爬上岸边来，偷吃田里的粮食，

fore, on Chinese New Year' s Eve, people living in the village would bring the old and the young to run away to the forest to shelter themselves from the monster named *Nian*.

以及农民家中的牲畜。有的时候，还经常伤害人的性命。因此，每当除夕这天，村里的人们都要携老扶幼，逃往森林之中，以躲避"年"的侵害。

Another New Year' s Eve had come again. People packed up in a hurry,led their own cattle and sheep and run away to the forest this morning. All of them were so scared that children could not stop crying and the elders who were loath to leave their hometown kept crying and shouting. At the moment, an old beggar appeared at the gateway of the village and begged food from people passing by. However, everyone was busy escaping and no one cared about him. For a while, an old woman who was on her way to escaping gave him some food and persuaded him to run into the forest immediately to elude *Nian* monster as she found him so poor.But the old beggar seemed not frightened at all. He just smiled and said, "You are such a kind-hearted old woman. Please allow me to live in your house this evening, I swear that I can help you to drive out the *Nian* monster." Hearing the promise, the old woman had a great surprise and said, "The monster is so terrible that you' d better run away instead of boasting yourself

又是一年除夕。这天早上，人们赶紧收拾好行装，牵着自家的牛和羊，纷纷开始逃往森林躲避。村里的人们都十分害怕，孩子们不停地哭泣，老人们则舍不得离开家，一直哭着喊着。就在这个时候，一个乞讨的老人出现在村口。他不停地向村口过往的人们索要食物。可是大家都忙着逃跑，根本就没有人理睬他。就在这时候，有一个准备逃跑的老奶奶看见了他。因为见他很可怜，所以给了他点食物，并劝他赶紧上山躲避"年"这个怪兽。那个乞讨的老人，似乎一点也不害怕，还微微地笑着说："好心的老奶奶，请让我在你家住上一个晚上吧，我一定帮你把'年'赶走。"老奶奶

!" Later the old woman went to the forest with others,leaving only the old beggar in the village.

Soon after it got dark, everywhere in the empty village was covered by darkness and silence. At that moment, the *Nian* monster came out, and searched for foods in an empty house. It ate all foods including corn, grain, fruits etc. in farmer's house and fed itself enough. It walked around the village as bold as brass, however, it found a lighted house. It was curious about knowing who dared to stay there instead of running. Actually the lighted house was the old woman's. When the monster saw the door with a big piece of red paper on it and the house was filled with bright light, it was frightened to shout out loudly. *Nian* was so angry that it swore to catch the guy, then it walked into the

一听，不由得大吃一惊，说道："这个怪兽可厉害了，你不要逞能了，还是赶紧逃命吧！"说完以后，老奶奶也跟着其他的人逃往森林去了。全村只留下了这个乞丐老人。

很快，夜幕就降临了。到处都是漆黑的一片，村里面也是静悄悄的，没有一个人。就在这时，"年"慢慢爬了出来。它来到一户人的家里，见到屋里没有人，便到处寻找食物吃。它将农民家中的玉米、粮食、瓜果等吃得一干二净，吃得很饱。它大摇大摆地在村里面走来走去，远处见到有一户人家的灯亮着。于是它想上去看个究竟，到底是谁这么大胆。这个还亮着灯的人家，就是老奶奶的家里。只看见老奶奶的家里灯火通明，门上贴着大红纸。"年"吓得大叫一声，当时很生气，它心想一定要将这个人抓住，于是又大胆地走进了院子。

yard. Suddenly, a crackling and spluttering sound made it startled and dare not go any further. It turned out that this monster was afraid of red color and fire light. At that moment the door of old woman's house was opened and there was an old guy with a red robe laughing loudly in the yard. As a result, *Nian* had to escape as soon as possible.

When it came to the following day, i.e. the first day of the first lunar month of the new year, people who had run away from the monster went back home from the forest. Everyone was so surprised that the village was kept the same as usual and then everyone joined in talking about the truth. At this point, the old woman recollected the experience of meeting the beggar and then told the whole event to villagers. Hearing the experience, the villagers were surprised and decided to take a look at the old woman's house. They found the door stuck with red paper, and the yard was left with the bamboos which weren't burnt out completely and the red candle was still lighting in the house. In order to celebrate the success of driving out the monster, the villagers put on new clothes and new hats, congratulating to relatives and friends. From then on, on every New Year's Eve, the gates of all fami-

就在这个时候，只听见噼里啪啦的响声，"年"吓得再也不敢走上前去了。原来它害怕红色与火光。这个时候，老奶奶家的大门被打开了，只见院子里有一个身披红袍的老人在哈哈大笑，"年"吓得很快就逃之夭夭了。

第二天，从森林里逃难的人们，又纷纷地跑回了家中。人们见村里面都安然无恙，大家十分惊奇，纷纷议论起来。就在这个时候，那个老奶奶才想起了昨天遇见乞丐的经过，便向乡亲们讲述了昨天发生的事。乡亲们听后都感到十分惊讶，纷纷跑到老奶奶家中去看个究竟。只见，老奶奶家门上贴着红纸，院子里有一大堆还没有燃烧殆尽的竹子，屋里面点燃的红蜡烛还在发着余光。乡亲们为了庆祝驱赶怪兽成功，纷纷穿上新衣服，戴着新帽子，向亲朋好友道喜问好。这件事很快在周围村

lies are put up on red antithetical couplet, and fireworks are set off on the arrival of the New Year. People like visiting relatives and friends to congratulate to each other the next day (the first day of first lunar month). This custom spreads more and more widely, becoming one of the most important traditional festivals in China.

子里传开了，人们都知道了驱赶“年”这种怪兽的方法。从此以后，每逢除夕夜晚，家家户户都贴着红对联，燃放爆竹，等待新年的到来。到第二天初一的时候，人们还要走亲访友，互相道喜问好。这个风俗便越传越广，成为中国最重要的传统节日之一。

Ⅱ. Customs

Family Reunion Dinner on New Year's Eve

New Year's Eve is the most important traditional festival and the moment of reunion. On that day, people have a dinner of a family reunion to welcome the arrival of the New Year. Even the relatives living far away will go back to celebrate the New Year.

It is also the busiest time on New Year's Eve. Women are busy cooking delicious cuisine for the evening banquet in the kitchen and men are busy cleaning the house completely and pasting the Spring Festival couplets. For children, it is time to have fun and they can set

二、习俗

年夜饭

除夕是中国人最重要的节日，也是一家团聚的重要时刻。这一天，人们要迎接新年，全家人在一起吃团圆饭。即便是远在外地的亲人，也要赶回家过年。

除夕也是大家最忙碌的时候。妇女们在厨房里忙着做各种美味佳肴，准备晚宴。男人们则忙着打扫屋子，贴春联，将家里打扫得干干净净。孩子

off fireworks and make a snowman. The dumpling is the necessary food on New Year's Eve. In the opinion of Chinese, Spring Festival cannot be perfect without having dumplings. On New Year's Eve, every family keeps busy cutting up meat and vegetables to make dumplings together. And the sound of firecrackers comes from the street. All the people put on new clothes with a smiling face and chat with each other so happily, creating an atmosphere filled with pleasure and joy.

Spring Festival Couplets

The Spring Festival couplet put up on the door is one of the most important customs on Spring Festival. The theme and content of Spring Festival couplets mainly includes celebrating the new year and a happy life. There is an interesting story about Spring Festival couplets in folk. Once upon a time, there were two brothers. They elaborately planted a range of peach trees.The elder brother was in charge of carrying water and hoeing, while the younger brother was responsible for pruning the branches and fertilizing beach trees. The neighbors living nearby appreciated the peaches and thought that those were the supernatural peaches. At that moment, a landowner wanted to eat the peach and believed that he could become immortal after having the peach. Then

们围在一起放鞭炮，堆雪人。饺子是大年三十最重要的食物。在中国人看来，如果过年不吃饺子，就不算是过年。除夕这天夜晚，家家户户都忙着剁肉、切菜,围坐在一起包饺子。大街上,传出的是阵阵爆竹声。所有人都穿着一新,面带笑容,有说有笑,洋溢出欢愉的气氛。

春联

春联是春节的时候,人们贴在门口的对联,是过春节最重要的习俗之一。春联的主题与内容,多以庆祝新年、祝福美好幸福的生活为主。民间还有一个关于春联的有趣故事。传说在很早以前,有两个兄弟,他们精心培育了一大片桃林,哥哥负责挑水、锄地,弟弟负责整理枝芽,给桃树施肥。住在附近的邻居,都十分赞赏兄弟俩种的桃子,说他们的桃子是仙桃。这个时候,有个地主想吃桃子,以为吃了桃子就可以

the landowner sent his servants to loot the peaches but they were totally defeated by the two brothers. However, the landowner's servants still didn't give up and they pretended to be the ghost to break through the peach forest to scare the brothers. However, the two brothers were not frightened at all and they cooperated to catch all these men. The elder brother used peach branches and the younger brother bundled a bunch of straw ropes. The two brother's heroic deeds were celebrated everywhere immediately, meanwhile they were renowned for miles around. However, the two brothers passed away soon. The neighbors who lived in and near the village felt sad and consoled themselves that the two brothers had gone to the heaven and been conferred immortals by Jade Emperor. People believed the peach trees they planted could be the protection against evil spirits. From then on, when came to the New Year's Eve, people would go to the peach forest and whittle two pieces of board from peach trees, and then draw the portraits of the two brothers on the board and hung them on the door to get rid of disasters and stun ghosts. This board made of peach trees is called Peach Amulet, which is developing into the Spring Festival couplet we are familiar with nowadays.

成仙,于是派他的手下来抢桃子,但很快被兄弟俩打得大败。一天夜晚,地主派手下扮成鬼怪,硬闯进桃林,企图吓走兄弟俩。可是兄弟俩并不害怕,哥哥手上拿起桃枝,弟弟抓起一捆草绳,将闯进桃林的人全部抓了起来。哥哥与弟弟勇斗盗匪的事迹很快就传开了,他们远近驰名。没过多久,兄弟俩去世了。周围的乡邻对他们的过世很难过。大家都说他们俩已经升入天堂,被玉皇大帝封为了神仙。大家都说他们兄弟俩种下的桃林,能够驱鬼辟邪。从此以后,每逢除夕之时,人们便纷纷去桃林削制两片桃木板,然后在上面画上兄弟俩的画像,挂在门板上,可以驱除灾祸,震慑鬼怪。这种桃制的木条被称为“桃符”,也就是现在人们所熟知的春联。

Paper-cut for Window Decoration

The so called paper-cut for window decoration is cutting red paper into a wide variety of shapes with the theme of human and animals and then paste them on the window. Both in the South and North, people always paste paper-cut on Spring Festival. Especially, in the country,almost all families put paper-cuts up on the window and door to show joys of the festival.

Greeting Cards

Nowadays sending greeting cards in New Year has become a popular custom in the every corner of the world. In western countries, sending cards has become a necessary celebrating rite on Christmas. Actually, when Spring Festival is coming, Chinese people present cards called Spring Greeting Cards to each other, too. Furthermore, China is the earliest country in which cards are invented and used. The Chinese ancient greeting cards originated from a kind of paper of personal visit, which was similar to the business cards at present. So on the occasion of Spring Festival, people would visit each other and give the best wishes. In order to introduce themselves to each other, they always gave a door paper to

剪窗花

所谓窗花，就是用红纸剪成各种主题的人物或动物，然后将其贴在窗户的玻璃上。无论在南方或是北方，每逢过年的时候，都要贴上窗花。尤其在农村，家家户户都要在窗户与门上贴窗花，以表现节日的喜庆气氛。

贺卡

如今在新年寄送贺卡已经成为世界各地流行的风俗。在西方，圣诞节送贺卡已经成为必备的庆祝仪式。事实上，在中国春节来临之际，人们也互赠贺卡，我们称之为“新春贺卡”。此外，中国也是最早发明并使用贺卡的国家。中国古代的贺卡源于一种拜门帖，类似于我们今天的名片。每逢新年之际，人们都要互相串门，致贺春节。为了向对方介绍自己，他们往往会递上一张门帖，以表明

show their identity. Meanwhile, there were some blessing words in the invitation expressing wishes and sharing joy about festival. Gradually the personal information on card has been reduced, on the contrary, people prefer writing blessing words instead of self-introduction. Now when it comes to Spring Festival, people still send each other greeting cards to give best wishes for the New Year.

自己的身份。为了向对方表示新年的祝贺，人们在门帖上还要写上几句祝福的话语，与大家共同分享节日快乐。慢慢的，贺卡上个人简介的信息逐渐淡化，反而是祝贺的话语越来越受到人们的重视。如今，每逢新年的时候，人们还要互送新春贺卡，给对方送上美好的新春祝福。

Pasting Chinese Characters Pronounced *Fu*

If you are careful enough, you can find that on Spring Festival, people always put a big Chinese characters pronounced *Fu* which means happiness and good luck on their doors. Pasting *Fu* has become a significant sign to celebrate Spring Festival. But foreigners are so confused that Chinese people put inverted *Fu* instead of regular shape of *Fu*. Actually in Chinese culture, pasting inverted *Fu* means the happiness and good luck are coming. Because in Chinese, coming pronounces the same as inverting. So the arrival

贴“福”字

如果你细心的话就会发现，每逢春节的时候，人们都要在自家门上贴上一个大大的“福”字。贴“福”字，已经成为庆祝新春的重要标志。可是令外国友人惊讶的是，为什么福字不是正的贴，而要倒着贴呢？在中国的传统文化中，“福”倒着贴，表示的是福到了的意思。因为在汉语中，“到”与“倒”的发音是相同的。

of *Fu* means that the happiness and good luck have been in your home.

Pasting New Year Pictures

The New Year picture is a form of Chinese paintings and also a representative for Chinese traditional craft. Most of traditional New Year pictures are carved by wood, which concentrates on glamorizing a kind of vivid atmosphere with vivid color. There are many themes of New Year pictures, such as flowers, birds, animals, fairy tales, legends or historical stories, expressing people's best wishes for a better life.

God of guarding the door is the common theme of a New Year picture. There is an interesting story about the god of guarding the door. It is said in the *Tang* Dynasty, a Dragon Emperor lived in the river located at suburb of *Chang'an*. Because the Dragon Emperor broke the rules of heaven, Jade Emperor commanded to behead the Dragon Emperor. The person executing the beheading was a famous official. Therefore, the Dragon Emperor asked for the absolution of his death from Emperor *Taizong* of *Tang*. One night when Emperor *Taizong* of

所谓福到了,就是指福气与幸运已经来到了你家。

贴年画

年画是中国画的一种形式,也是中国传统工艺的代表。传统的年画主要以木刻为主,着力渲染一种热闹的氛围,色彩鲜明。年画的主题也很多,有花卉、鸟类、动物、神话传说或历史故事等,表达了人们祈祷美好生活的夙愿。

门神是常见的年画主题。有关门神的由来,还有一段有趣的故事。据说在唐朝的时候,在都城长安郊外的河里住着一个龙王。由于这个龙王违反了天规,玉皇大帝降旨将其斩首。执行斩首的人是唐太宗身边一个有名的大臣。于是,龙王就去求唐太宗,请唐太宗免它一死。一天深夜,唐太宗呼呼大睡,这个龙王闯入

Tang had fallen asleep deeply, the Dragon Emperor broke into his dream and described the cause of the whole event. Emperor *Taizong* of *Tang* expressed great sympathy for Dragon Emperor' s experience and promised to absolve him. However, the official still beheaded Dragon Emperor on the day set by Jade Emperor. Later the Dragon Emperor became a ghost and prepared to make a death threat to Emperor *Taizong* of *Tang*. Consequently Emperor *Taizong* of *Tang* was too scared to fall asleep. In order to reduce Emperor' s suffering, the official ordered two generals to stand out of the palace for a whole night to protect Emperor. From then on, the Dragon Emperor' s ghost never dare to disturb the Emperor. This story was spread among the folk soon. The common people want to get safety, so they draw the portraits of these two generals and paste them on their doors to get rid of ghosts and monsters.

了唐太宗的梦中，并将事情的缘由告诉了唐太宗。唐太宗十分同情龙王的遭遇，答应免去龙王的死罪。唐太宗身边的大臣，却还是在玉皇大帝规定的日子将龙王斩首了。龙王变成了鬼，准备向唐太宗索命。唐太宗惊吓过度，整天晚上都睡不着觉。这个大臣为了缓解唐太宗的痛苦，命唐太宗手下的两位大将军，整夜都站在皇宫门口，守卫唐太宗。此后，这个龙王再也不敢来骚扰唐太宗了。这个故事很快在民间广为流传。老百姓为了保佑平安，将两位将军的样子画了下来，贴在自家的门上，以躲避妖魔鬼怪。

Eating New Year Cake

In the Chinese southern part, on every Spring Festival, people need to have New Year cakes made of glutinous rice flour. The flavors of New Year cakes can be divided into northern and southern ones. Actually, the flavor of southern New Year cake is much more delicious. The best flavor of southern New

吃年糕

在中国的南方，每逢过年的时候，人们都要吃年糕。年糕分为南北两种风味，但就口味上而言，南方年糕的口感更好。南方年糕主要以苏州、广东、宁波这三个地方的最好。味

Year cake is distributed in *Suzhou*, *Guangdong* and *Ningbo*. There are three chief tastes, salty, sweet and flavorless. In addition, there are many cooking methods such as steaming, frying, boiling and stir baking, which do deserve to be the delicious Chinese cuisine.

道主要有咸味的、甜味的以及无味的。在烹饪手法上，可以蒸、炸、煮、炒等，不愧是中华美食。

Wandering the Temple Fair

In order to go shopping conveniently, people always choose to wander the temple fair which refers to the party near the temple in which the activities of worshipping, shopping or entertainment are held. It is a kind of festival custom with Chinese traditional culture. The temple fair relates to religion rites. During the period of South and North Dynasties, all dominators of that time believed in Buddhism so that they built temples everywhere. When great religious activities were held in the temple, people would come and go from all directions. The vendors would display their goods on both sides of the roads to the temple for the provisions for visitors and believers, which became the temple fair gradually. In the temple fair, there are varieties of booths such as food booths and goods booths. Meanwhile there is also the performance of jugglery and traditional Chinese opera to create a happy atmosphere. Later the temple fair becomes an activity including the performance with folk culture.

逛庙会

为了方便采办年货，人们往往在过年的时候，要去逛庙会。庙会，指的是在寺庙附近聚会，进行祭神、购物或娱乐等活动，是颇具中国传统文化的一种节日风俗。庙会与宗教仪式有关。在南北朝时期，当时的统治者都信奉佛教，到处建造寺庙。每逢寺庙举行盛大宗教活动的时候，人们都要从四面八方赶来。商贩们为了给游人与信徒提供货物，于是将自己的商品摆在前往寺院的两旁，遂形成了庙市。庙市上会摆放着各种饮食摊、货摊，还有一些助兴的杂耍曲艺表演等，从而形成了以民俗文化表演为主的活动。随着时代的变化，庙会的

With the change of times, there is a huge change about the temple fair's forms. Besides business activities in the temple fair, lion dance, flower exhibition, handcraft show, book exhibition with discounted price, Chinese traditional opera, martial art, acrobatics and other special activities are held, which has become a place integrating traveling and visiting with entertainment.

形式也发生了很大的变化。除了商业活动外，还要举办舞狮、花卉展、手工艺展、特价书展、京剧、武术、杂技等活动，成为集旅游观光、休闲娱乐于一体的场所。

CPSIA information can be obtained
at www.ICGtesting.com
Printed in the USA
BVHW01*0931220718
521998BV00022B/25/P

9 781921 816550